GET THAT MONKEY OFF MY BACK

GENE PIKE

BIBLICAL AND PRACTICAL KEYS TO GET OUT OF DEBT AND STAY OUT

GET THAT MONKEY OFF MY BACK

TATE PUBLISHING
AND ENTERPRISES, LLC

Get That Monkey off My Back
Copyright © 2013 by Gene Pike. All rights reserved.

No part of this publication may be reproduced, stored in a retrieval system or transmitted in any way by any means, electronic, mechanical, photocopy, recording or otherwise without the prior permission of the author except as provided by USA copyright law.

Scripture quotations are taken from the Holy Bible, King James Version, Cambridge, 1769. Used by permission. All rights reserved.

This book is designed to provide accurate and authoritative information with regard to the subject matter covered. This information is given with the understanding that neither the author nor Tate Publishing, LLC is engaged in rendering legal, professional advice. Since the details of your situation are fact dependent, you should additionally seek the services of a competent professional.

The opinions expressed by the author are not necessarily those of Tate Publishing, LLC.

Published by Tate Publishing & Enterprises, LLC
127 E. Trade Center Terrace | Mustang, Oklahoma 73064 USA
1.888.361.9473 | www.tatepublishing.com

Tate Publishing is committed to excellence in the publishing industry. The company reflects the philosophy established by the founders, based on Psalm 68:11,
"*The Lord gave the word and great was the company of those who published it.*"

Book design copyright © 2013 by Tate Publishing, LLC. All rights reserved.
Cover design by Jan Sunday Quilaquil
Interior design by Honeylette Pino

Published in the United States of America
ISBN: 978-1-62510-833-3
1. Religion / General
2. Business & Economics / General
13.06.12

DEDICATION

To our grandchildren, in hope they will experience the blessings and joys of living within their financial means all the days of their lives rather than the bondage of debt.

ACKNOWLEDGMENTS

> Render therefore to all their dues: tribute to whom tribute is due; custom to whom custom; fear to whom fear; honour to whom honour.
>
> Romans 13:7 (KJV)

First, I would like to praise God for he is true to his word! He has never left me or forsaken me! He has revealed himself to me more so in the valleys than on the mountain tops. He is always with me. He is my help in times of trouble. He is my comforter and my hope.

Second, I give honor to my wonderful wife, Ann. From day one, she insisted that if I was going to date her, I would have to go to church with her. Because of Ann, I reestablished a vital relationship with God that has strengthened through the trials of life. She has suffered and prevailed through a lot of my early bad decisions. She has faithfully stood by my side for nearly forty-three years at the time of writing this book. I honor her for contributing to the section on wisdom of purchasing.

Third, I would like to give honor to my parents and my children. My parents gave me sacrificial love and instilled in me the values of respect, honesty, and giving. I honor my wonderful children; my daughter, Angela, and her husband, Allen Eckman; my son Christopher and his wife, Shelly; my son Dustin and his wife, Kristin; and my beautiful grandchildren—children of Allen and Angela: Ashlynd, Logan, and Winter Eckman; children of Christopher and Shelly: Mitchell, Kathryn, and Samuel Pike; children of Dustin and Kristin: Kylie and Zachary Pike for their love and support. They bring such joy into my life.

I give honor to all of my pastors through the years for their encouragement and for laying a strong, biblical foundation for my walk with God. I give honor to my current pastor, Bishop Gary Adkins, who has always shown me the greatest of respect and is one of the best communicators of all the ministers I know. He can keep your attention saying more in forty minutes than many ministers can say in two hours. He has helped me to greatly improve the content and delivery of the messages I preach.

I especially honor two of the most godly men that I have ever known who have greatly influenced my life with their teaching, discernment, integrity, counsel, and their personal walk with God. Both of these men have and will continue to sacrifice everything to maintain the scriptural truths of God's word, and they have impacted my Christian walk more than any other men I have ever known. They are my special friends Bishop Kenneth Dale Baker and Jim Gilbraith II. Together they have helped counsel and guide me and my family during some very difficult years of our life. As my former pastor, Bishop Baker was the first to present the teachings of Larry Burkett. He gave me my first counselees to teach about biblical finances. He is one of wisest men I know and has the deepest insight about scripture of any minister I have heard preach and/or teach. His preaching encouraged me to dig deep into the whole word of God and seek revelation and inspiration from God. He has a heart for people and is uncompromising of God's word. Jim Gilbraith II is also one of the wisest men I know, and he, too, has a tremendous heart for God and people. Though he is not a licensed minister, he is a minister's teacher and has a great command of scripture, and understanding and God given discernment. Jim truly cares about people and pleasing God! He has demonstrated to me the reality that "it is more blessed to give than to receive," and "you can't out give God!" I'm honored that both Bishop Baker and Jim Gilbraith II are my good friends and personal counselors.

I also honor the late Larry Burkett whom I consider the pioneer on promoting debt-free living. I hold his work in great esteem as I have used some modifications of his materials in my counseling ministry. Also, I give honor to Crown Ministries and Dave Ramsey for their ministries and materials that have helped me to assist others to become debt-free. I give honor to Cheryl Cochrane who has encouraged me and tirelessly edited the rough manuscript of this book. I give honor to Robbie Sistar for his contribution of photographs and original inspiration for a book cover.

I give to God all of the honor and the glory! Amen.

CONTENTS

Success Stories 13
Introduction 21
What God Did for Us, He Desires to Do for You 27
Life Lessons 33
Get Out of Debt: God's Plan 61
Spiritual Keys for Getting Out of Debt 85
Practical Keys for Getting Out of Debt 105
Buying With Wisdom 141
Planning Wisdom 183
Educate Your Children about Financial Matters 187
Addendum 213
Endnotes 233

SUCCESS STORIES

I'm amazed how God works in our lives when we are faithful to apply the wisdom he gives in his word. From the many individuals we have counseled, the following two testimonies are examples of the success individuals have experienced in a short period of time applying biblical principles and practical applications taught in this book. With their permission, I am including their personal testimonies.

They received no compensation for their contribution to this book.

APRIL STEVENS

April is a single mom who came to me struggling to organize her finances. Using spreadsheets similar to those in the back of this book, we compiled her financial information and developed a life financial plan. I gave her some basic instructions and met with her several times over a few months to evaluate progress and to make adjustments. She listened and followed the instructions, and God blessed her by allowing her to reach her goals sooner than she expected! The following is April's testimony:

> I first came to know about a "budget" through Brother Gene Pike and my church at Harvest Ministries in Rock Hill, SC. My goal was to pay off my two automobiles. In addition, my daughter had started college so I had those expenses as well. I spoke to Brother Pike about helping me organize a budget plan. I thought about getting a part-time job as a waitress during the evenings and on weekends, and I actually started that in August of 2010. This was all part of God's plan. My son and I went into a local pizza place, and there was a sign, "hiring for a waitress." During dinner, my son gave me a letter from

USC-Columbia which included the tuition costs for my daughter's college so I said, "I definitely need to get a job!" I walked out of the restaurant, and I looked back at the sign for "hiring for a waitress." I told my son, "I am going to apply." I walked back in and spoke to the manager who said, "Can you start this week?" I said, "Thank you, I will be here." What a testimony! Although it was tiring for me working seven days a week, I was determined to accomplish my goals.

What I did was to weed away all the unnecessary expenses I didn't need. For instance, cable TV went to basic which saved about $40.00 a month. I disconnected the internet at home which saved $60.00 plus. Coupons were my favorite hobby. I would purchase two newspapers and go through all the store ads to get the better deals. Of course I watched for the double or triple coupons because they were the best. When the cashier gave me my receipt at the end of the order, it was great to see the reward of the monies saved.

Brother Pike explained to me to first start paying off the vehicle I owed the least on. I realized that if I paid the monthly payment earlier than the due date that the daily interest that accrues for the amount of days that are paid early went toward the principle of the loan. I paid the payment earlier than the due date which assisted me in paying the loan off earlier than I expected, and then I started on the other vehicle. I owed around $15,000 plus a mortgage when I started the budget and started paying off the vehicles. I paid off my Ford in February of 2011 and then the Honda in May 2011. I just recently quit my waitress position. Regarding the college expenses, I have paid off my daughter's first year of college which amounted to about $9,000.

I can't thank Brother Pike enough for his blessings upon my changed life style. By the grace of God and the wisdom of Brother Pike, I followed these simple principles and was able to be debt free and only have a mortgage to pay.

I'm now concentrating on paying off the mortgage early. Thank you for your generosity for sharing your knowledge Brother Pike.

KENNY AND MARIE PROCTOR

Kenny and Marie first approached me shortly after they were married. I remember after compiling their financial information, I said under my breath, "God, if you don't help me, I don't know what I will tell them to do." However, with God's help, we were able to develop a workable plan. We set a follow-up appointment with instructions for them to notify me if anything changed about their financial situation. The following is their testimony presented to the author by e-mail attachment and with their approval was corrected grammatically and for accuracy of content for publication in this book.

> Here are just a few things we'd like to share that we have learned, and how God has moved in our life financially, spiritually, and in our family. We do not mind if you copy our testimony and share it with others.
>
> As long as we have been Christians we have always tithed. It wasn't until we learned the following principles that we put ourselves in the driver's seat of seeking to be debt free and what it would consist of….

PSALM 24:1 PRINCIPLE OF OWNERSHIP

Tithing. God gets the first fruits because it belongs to him. We tithe on 'gross' income rather than 'net'.

Once we realized that everything belongs to the Lord, we were able to view our financial situation in the right perspective.

LUKE 16:10 PRINCIPLE OF STEWARDSHIP

Examples of being faithful in tithing and of being unjust:
- *Faithful in tithing*: Our overall testimony (If we would have chose not to tithe, then we would have chosen to

remove ourselves from God's covering so withholding tithes was not an option for us if we wanted God's help!)
- *Unjust*: A "bootleg" movie was given to us to watch. Instead of giving it back we thought we'd watch it and buy the original later…well, our DVD player ended up breaking after the movie! We learned that if we wanted God's blessing in our lives especially financially, we would have to always walk in integrity! Another example is someone wanted to bless us with food, and it was purchased with their food-stamps. I thought it would be fine because it was their blessing to us and besides, we could use a break on our personal food budget. At the end of the month, our food budget was double the expense it generally was, and it was to the exact dollar amount over that was spent using someone's food-stamps. This was a hard lesson to learn because I didn't want to hurt the individual's feelings and make them feel like we had a "better than" attitude. We learned that what should have happened was to say, "No, thanks. We can't use government funding that isn't legally ours." Who knows, perhaps our integrity could have helped the other person in the long run.

LUKE 16:11 PRINCIPLE OF MINISTRY

We never knew finances could be so spiritual. We've learned that being bound in the physical matters binds us in the spiritual matters, but when we are free in the physical realm (or at least working to be debt free) we are free to move as God would have us in the spiritual realm.

In beginning our budget in June 2006 (a few weeks after we were married), we realized our total debt was $44,000. Marie Home Depot -$3,500, Marie visa card -$1,800, Kenny visa card -$1,000, Kenny credit card -$4,000, Kenny car loan -$4,000, Kenny Student loan -$28,500, Kenny Student loan -$1,200. Our combined income was only $2800 a month. We had to cut out all extra's just to pay all bills and debt. No More Credit Card! We cut all of them up!

Below is a history of events we encountered as we put those principles to use.

TITHE FIRST, NO MATTER WHAT!

- As soon as we made a commitment to budget and get out of debt, God blessed us by making a way for Kenny's car to be paid off. ($4,000)
- July 2006. We found out I was pregnant! (Brother Pike said in our first counseling session, "Whatever you do, don't get pregnant right away"). Wow! We took a deep breath and trusted that God would see us through if we stayed faithful to him through budgeting. After all, children are only as expensive as you make them! Then we told Brother Pike: One student loan was deferred and cancelled! ($1,200)
- August 2006. Kenny started a new job teaching where he was able to make extra money by coaching. This was another blessing.
- December 2006. Our washer broke and our dryer was burning our clothes. We purchased both units for $830 cash!
- March 2007. Kenny's parents blessed us with a gift of $200 and told us that we couldn't use any of it to pay bills with. We had to use it as entertainment money. We didn't pay bills with it, but we couldn't justify spending $200 for entertainment either so we rented a movie, went out to eat, and put the rest in savings!
- Mia, our 2nd child was born! And along with her came doctor bills! One week later I broke my little toe, and 2 weeks after that I had an emergency appendectomy. So, we had even more doctor bills. And to top it off, out of 6 weeks of maternity leave I was only getting paid for 2 weeks! Ouch!

- Received a $3,600 tax return that went right to pay off a credit card.
- April 2007. I was supposed to go back to work and logically, with all the medical bills and don't forget debt, I needed to go back to work. After praying a long while about staying home or returning to work, we decided it would be best for me to stay home.
- May 2007. We were blessed again with a $100 gift.
- Our local Technical College called me to teach for the summer session -8 weeks -2 nights a week ($1,700)
- June 2007. All the doctor bills started rolling in. We were able to pay the debt to all the doctors, hospital and labs in full!
- We were blessed again with a $50 gift.
- July 2007. We were blessed again with a $200 gift specified to spend on tires.
- August 2007. Kenny had wisdom teeth removed. (paid in full $700 cash after insurance paid)
- November 2007. Another gift of $100

In addition to all the small monetary gifts, we also received hand-me-down clothing for both Macie & Mia! I was even able to wear some of the clothes intended for Macie! We were also blessed with $20 here and $10 there for diapers! And, we tithed on everything! What a blessing! We continued to pray for "little jobs" and that is what we got: E-bay sales, Kenny's band, cleaning houses, occasional babysitting, Auto Cad jobs, yard sales, consignment sales, cleaning up yards and garages, helping cater, teaching / preaching.

By February 2008 (20 months after we began budgeting), we were able to clear $20,000 in debt by following Godly principles! Our 2006 income amounted to $51,000 with both of us working! Our 2007 income was $47,481. Kenny worked all year with me choosing to stay at home and working all our little jobs! Needless to say, we adjusted our budget 13 times in 21 months! We wanted to make sure we were doing all that we could!

Where we are today: August 2012 (4 ½ years later).

- God has blessed us with 2 more children (April 2009 & November 2011) in which the hospital and doctor bills were paid in full prior to delivery making a total of 4 children.
- Kenny completed his Masters Degree which we paid cash for as he took one class at a time ($18,000)
- As our family grew we had to upsize on vehicles! We bought three used vehicles and paid cash for them ($16,000) and gave our other three vehicles away in good condition.
- I was hired at the church in July 2010 which provided a little more income.
- June of 2012, Kenny took a job that paid $17,000 less per year; however, we are still making a little more than we did when we first got married!
  - Debt:
  - Mortgage
  - Student loan ($13,000)

All of our praise goes to God who continues to see us through this *debt-free* process. He was able to work through Brother Gene Pike who taught us biblical principles on finances. When we first met with Brother Pike, our situation was as hopeless as one can imagine although being young and in love we didn't realize that our debt was huge! We were just determined that it was going to work, and we were going to be debt free and not live in bondage on credit or government assistance. We are looking forward to that day when we can be totally debt free!

Thank you, Brother Pike, for your patience and encouragement for the last six years, and for allowing the Lord to use you in such a powerful way. Your calling is a gift from God and you fulfill it well!

INTRODUCTION

Monkeys are really cute and an exciting part of most zoos. As a child, I can remember asking my parents for a real monkey. I got a stuffed one! They agreed monkeys are cute, but as adults, they realized monkeys were messy and would be a burden to keep. They also realized the potential dangers associated with monkeys. So, for my welfare and theirs, they wisely said no to my request. Likewise, the initial benefits you receive from debt can look good and can be exciting, but, if only you could have foreseen the mess, the burden and the dangers associated with debt, you, like my parents, would have probably said no to debt.

No matter how cute that monkey was, can you image carrying a monkey on your back twenty-four hours a day? What a burden! Do you feel like you are carrying a heavy debt load on your back? You have tried taking it off, and it just keeps coming back! It's a debt monkey! When you are heavily in debt, you are carrying an unnecessary load that wears down your spirit, your mind, your emotions, and your physical body. My wife Ann and I know this from our personal experience with debt, and we know this was never God's plan for us or for you!

Well, it's time to get that monkey off your back! Not just for a moment, but for the rest of your life. It can be a reality! It will not take a life time to become debt-free!

I can't describe the relief I experienced the day I was completely out of debt. Since that period of time I have devoted much of my ministry to helping others attain this same goal and enjoy what Ann and I have experienced in becoming debt-free and staying debt-free.

I'm not promoting that you will get financially rich by being out of debt, but you certainly will have a peace beyond natural reason. You will no longer be in financial bondage. You will be free!

Together with my wife, we present this book from our life experiences as a tool to help change your habits and the way you think financially! You can and will be set free from the bondage of debt when you develop new habits, and your thinking elevates to the correct spiritual position. You will be like my parents concerning the monkey—wise to the responsibilities, burdens, and dangers associated with debt. You will have knowledge to make wise financial choices!

Always remember God and his written words are your first resources for help! God was my direct source of instructions from the beginning! He spoke! I listened! I obeyed! This is key to your success in life! I was a good Christian who paid my tithes, and gave offerings, and was faithful, and active in my local church; however, I was heavily in debt like most Americans until God showed me the way out. I had read the Old Testament four times and the New Testament at least seven times! But I had a wow experience with God's word after I got out of debt. My church was offering a Wednesday-night class using Larry Burkett's material. It was exciting to me as he pointed out the very scriptures that showed the principles God had spoken into my spirit months previously. These scriptures became alive to me, and they will to you, too! When God speaks something into your spirit, it never leaves you, and his written word jumps off the pages and becomes alive!

Let there be no doubt, God is the author and finisher of my faith. I make no apologies for the spiritual intent and context of this book. First and foremost, God has called us to have a personal and intimate relationship with him through his son, Jesus Christ. Nothing else is more important than for you to give your heart and life to him. God had a purpose for your creation and desires to bless you!

> And we know that all things work together for good to them that love God, to them who are the called according to his purpose.
>
> Romans 8:28 (KJV)

> Who hath saved us, and called us with an holy calling, not according to our works, but according to his own purpose and grace, which was given us in Christ Jesus before the world began.
>
> 2 Timothy 1:9 (KJV)

Even if you are not a Christian, you will greatly benefit by applying what is revealed in this book. However, I encourage you to maximize the benefits by accepting Jesus Christ not only in your heart but to become Lord of your life. Too many ask Jesus into their heart but fail to let him be Lord of their lives. It doesn't work! You will never fulfill what God desires through your life and will only experience defeat after defeat and, ultimately, his judgment in eternity.

As Christians, we must not take lightly the word of God, and we must heed James's warning!

> But be ye doers of the word, and not hearers only, deceiving your own selves.
>
> James 1:22 (KJV)

It is only when we apply his word in our daily lives that we experience the joy, peace, and blessings of God, and then we truly understand the power of his written word. Read his word daily and apply it, and you will see what I mean.

I thank God for Ann! She is, first, my helpmeet and, second, a vital part of this ministry. We married on November 22, 1970, and have three children, their spouses, and eight beautiful grandchildren at the writing of this book. At the age of thirteen, Ann became active in our local church in the children's ministries programs serving as a teacher and ultimately the director of the children's ministry. She also has served as director of many of the wonderful Children's Christmas programs at our local church throughout the years. She believes and practices that if it's worth doing, it's worth doing right. I'm so proud of what she has accomplished over the years even with very little funds given to her to operate these ministries. Now she is devoting her time to our grandchildren and this ministry while continuing a part time career of twenty-eight years with the city of Rock Hill, South Carolina Parks and Recreational Department as arts programmer.

I also have been involved in various ministries of my local church since the age of eighteen. I will go into more detail later in my testimony. Recently, I retired from the leadership positions I held in my local church to pursue my heart's desire to write and expand our ministry to others outside of my local church. Currently, I am the general director of Life Ministries, a minister, teacher, counselor, and a missionary to Peru.

In the developmental stage of this book, Ann asked me the question, "With so many books about getting out of debt on the market, why would someone buy your book?" This is a good question, and the answer was simple! It is because, my book not only teaches principles which are extremely important, but gives detailed Bible-based common sense and practical keys on just how to get out of debt and stay out of debt! What I present in this book is what God gave me during our financial crisis, and the principles and practical keys were effective in making us debt-free.

By implementing the biblical principles and practical keys in this book, you could be debt-free in thirty-six months or less excluding your mortgage, and mortgages could be paid off in less than 50 percent of the remaining contract time saving tens of thousands of dollars in interest. I know this because of my personal experience and the testimonies of those that have fully followed my advice in counseling.

The opinions I state in this book are my opinions. I have a right to my own opinions. You can have a different opinion and that's okay with me, but how is your opinion working for you? Are you debt-free? I am! Let me say that God's mind far exceeds ours, and his ways are greater than ours.

> For my thoughts are not your thoughts, neither are your ways my ways, saith the LORD. For as the heavens are higher than the earth, so are my ways higher than your ways, and my thoughts than your thoughts.
>
> Isaiah 55:8–9 (KJV)

It is clear we need the mind of God if we are going to do the right things the right way. Everyone has an opinion, but what God thinks and says is what is right and what is important. I can only share what I have learned, but God must speak truth into your mind and heart, and he will if you will only ask him.

This book is not intended to be exclusive in dealing with every spiritual condition and/or every personal debt situation, it does not address the details of every financial plan or program available in today's market; in fact, God's thoughts and ways are often completely opposite of the views of the secular minds of the business world. Therefore, I advise seeking knowledge and wisdom from godly men that are knowledgeable in the details of the various plans and programs available today for specific needs beyond every day debt management (i.e., estate planning, college funds, etc.). Fasting and prayer was essential for preparing my heart to hear and understand the principles and practical keys God taught me. Like me, you will need a personal word from God for your situation. Only he can instill in your heart the spiritual understanding of the principles and practical keys he gave me. Otherwise, you will not remain committed to apply them to get out of debt and to stay out of debt. Again, I stress that it is essential you hear from God concerning your personal situation. You are not just fighting a physical battle, but a spiritual war. How we manage wealth is a window to the spiritual condition of our heart! You need spiritual counsel for spiritual needs. Therefore, in addition to this book, I advise you to seek the wisdom, and submit to the authority, of your pastor, a minister, or a godly counselor.

Apply the principles and practical keys taught in this book, and you, too, can have a testimony of God's mercy, grace, and divine intervention in the financial areas of your life.

Since I first started sharing what God taught me and Ann about becoming debt-free, it has been my heart that those I have personally counseled would one day also counsel others to become debt-free. No matter how much I might desire to, I can't counsel everyone! But you can impact the lives of those around you by sharing your life experiences, and the lessons you have learned as you put the principles and practical keys into action!

God worked many miracles during our process of becoming debt-free, and I will share some of those in this book. I believe he will do the same for you.

I would like to hear your personal testimony of your experience in becoming debt-free. Send your testimony by e-mail to Life Ministries or directly to me Gene W. Pike.[1]

WHAT GOD DID FOR US, HE DESIRES TO DO FOR YOU

Ann and I have been where some of you are today with bills exceeding your income! Dealing with bill collectors calling all hours of the day and night! Working two or more jobs day and night to survive. Not being able to stay at home from work to recover from sickness! We understand the bondage and pressure you are under. We were at the point of bankruptcy until we heard from God! With a shout of joy and praise to our Lord, today we are debt-free!

Let me assure you that you can be debt-free! If God did it for us, he will do it for you. I truly believe God does not love Ann and me anymore than he loves you. What he did for us he will do for you if you will listen and obey!

We offer no magical formula and no ten step process to get out of debt in this book! What we do offer are some simple biblical principles and practical keys that God showed me to get out of debt! They worked for Ann and me, and they will work for you, if you will apply them! Since 1986, we have shared theses keys in our counseling ministry. Those that applied these keys have experienced similar results as Ann and I experienced.

I will tell you that by faithfully applying what we teach, you could be debt-free with the exception of your mortgage in thirty-six months or less, and mortgages could be paid off in less than 50 percent of the remaining contract time, saving tens of thousands of dollars that can be used to live blessed lives and to invest into God's kingdom. Just imagine what you could do with $50,000 or more in your bank account. This could be possible by simply eliminating interest on your home, vehicles, and credit cards, etc. How, would you like paying cash for your next car, your next vacation, your children's education, and your children's wedding? Would you like having substantial savings to pay for life circumstances or supplement your retirement? All this is possible, and we will give you the necessary keys in this book to make it possible. You must become debt-free to experience these blessings!

Would you really be interested in knowing how to be totally debt-free?

Well, it can happen; but it requires hearing Godly instruction, an attitude change, commitment, discipline, and obedience! Failing to maintain any one of these consistently for the rest of your life will result in only short term freedom. You will return to your old ways, and return to the bondage of debt. I believe what Peter says about backsliding is appropriate.

> But it is happened unto them according to the true proverb, The dog is turned to his own vomit again; and the sow that was washed to her wallowing in the mire.
>
> 2 Peter 2:22 (KJV)

Not a pretty picture! Is this really what you desire? Being debt-free and living within your means requires commitment and discipline? It is not half hearted, but sold out to the concept of living within your means and allowing God to bless you, so that you may bless others.

It is our heart for you to have a lifetime experience of achieving debt-free living, passing your experience and this knowledge to your next generation, and so others may see your life and the associated peace and joy of living debt-free.

Hear me well, God has a plan for your life and any wealth he entrust unto you! Being in debt bondage hinders your ability to fulfill God's purpose in your life. It is not God's plan for you to be in debt, full of fear with the associated frustrations, and suffering. God desires to meet your needs and give you peace and joy!

How we use money or wealth is important to God. There are more than two thousand Scriptures associated with wealth. It is important that we understand God's purpose for money. The late Larry Burkett taught and God's word confirms that God has three primary purposes for wealth. These purposes in their proper order are to *serve* God, to meet our personal needs, and to meet the needs of others. Committing to faithfully administer disbursements of money toward these purposes and applying God's principles of stewardship brings peace to our minds, contentment with what we have, joy in giving, and can allow surplus money for the purpose of fulfilling reasonable wants and desires and to meet the needs of others.

Failing to administer money according to God's priority reveals a spiritual problem and will result in many unnecessary difficulties in this life. Sadly, many Christian's are carnally minded, and so they fail to administer money according to God's purpose. The carnal mind focuses on self. The carnal mind seeks to fulfill wants and desires with little or no priority to God's ministries and the needs of others. The carnal mind must have that big house, expensive cars, boats, vacations, designer clothes, the latest electronic gadget, and the list goes on.

Learn this lesson well: You can't find true fulfillment in these things. God says,

> Hell and destruction are never full; so the eyes of man are never satisfied.
>
> Proverbs 27:20 (KJV)

Again, You will never find satisfaction in things! Satisfaction only comes through your relationship with God and fulfilling God's purpose for your life!

> My praise shall be of thee in the great congregation: I will pay my vows before them that fear him. The meek shall eat and be satisfied: they shall praise the LORD that seek him: your heart shall live for ever.
>
> Psalm 22:25–26 (KJV)

> How excellent is thy lovingkindness, O God! therefore the children of men put their trust under the shadow of thy wings. They shall be abundantly satisfied with the fatness of thy house; and thou shalt make them drink of the river of thy pleasures.
>
> Psalm 36:7–8 (KJV)

Don't get me wrong. There is nothing wrong with desires and wants as long as our attitude and actions are in alignment with God's word.

If we faithfully follow God's plans for wealth, God can also allow an additional surplus to fulfill some reasonable wants and desires. However, many people fail to administer money according to God's plan, putting their wants and desires above God's ministries and the needs of others. This ultimately leads to God's judgment; hopefully it is in this life versus eternity!

If there is one thing I have learned, it is that God's word is true: You will reap what you sow!

> Be not deceived; God is not mocked: for whatsoever a man soweth, that shall he also reap. For he that soweth to his flesh shall of the flesh reap corruption; but he that soweth to the Spirit shall of the Spirit reap life everlasting.
>
> Galatians 6:7–8 (KJV)

This passage of Scripture not only deals with eternity, but its application definitely affects every aspect of our present lives. I really like the ninth verse which says the following:

> And let us not be weary in well doing: for in due season we shall reap, if we faint not.
>
> Galatians 6:9 (KJV)

Almost everyone that comes to me wants me to immediately fix their financial problem. The truth is that for most situations, I could pay off all the debts, and eighteen to thirty-six months later, they would be in the same financial condition. Why? Because debt is an indicator of a spiritual problem! I'm not trying to be mean, I'm being truthful. You can't permanently fix the physical until you fix the spiritual. We will address this in more detail later in this book.

Let me say this, don't expect to get out of debt tomorrow! You did not get in debt overnight! Getting out of debt is like surgery; it's necessary, it's painful, it takes time to recover, and it cost you something, but in the end, you will be healed. There is victory for those that endure!

I know people that reap pain, sorrow, uncertainty, and lack of provision because of wrong attitudes and actions. They live their lives in misery and they lack hope of ever having freedom. They are like the mule tied to the molasses mill going in a circle all day, resting at night only to return to the same routine day after day. When you are in this routine circle of debt there really is no relief at night when you lay down to sleep. You arise to another day of debt that often multiplies beyond reasonable hope. But I'm here to tell you there is hope! Jesus is your hope! He is the God of knowledge, truth, grace, mercy, and life. He has the answers to your problems, and he will intervene in your behalf if only you will hear him speak, listen to his instructions, and obey. Again, this is key to success in every aspect of your life!

I also know those that reap great pleasures and desires above their needs because their attitudes and actions are in alignment with God's word. I have a friend that applies God's heart in all three purposes for wealth. He gives more to help people and to the ministry than most church's budget for the poor and for mission work. Yet he lacks nothing; the more he gives, the more God gives him. God can do this because God knows his heart! God has tried him, and he has proven that he is faithful. Everything he sets his hands upon is blessed. He blesses, and he reaps blessings! Would you like this to be said of you? Well, it can, but it will require change!

> And be not conformed to this world: but be ye transformed by the renewing of your mind, that ye may prove what is that good, and acceptable, and perfect, will of God.
>
> Romans 12:2 (KJV)

Hear me! You are going to reap whatever you have sown, but the choice of what you reap is dependent upon you!

Again, I repeat, how we manage money is an indicator of the spiritual condition of our heart. Debt is a *symptom* not the problem. In our society, we try to fix the symptom rather than the problem. The media is full of advertisements to fix your debt problems. The truth is that what you get is temporary relief from the symptom, but the pain returns and their bank accounts are richer. We have a pill for every ache and pain, but pills often only mask the real problem. Sometimes we need surgery. When it comes to debt, we need spiritual surgery to transform our actions. God desires and is willing to operate so that you can be healed. Just ask him to do it! He did it for Ann and me, and he will do it for you because he does not love us any more than he loves you!

Pray this prayer before proceeding to the next chapter,

> Father, I need your healing. Come into my heart and be Lord of my life. Give me the desire to renew my mind through the sanctifying power of your word. Let me hunger and thirst after your righteousness that I might be filled, that I might be healed, that I might be transformed, that I might do that which is right according to your word. I commit that from this moment on I will seek to know you and to know your ways. I will dedicate my life to applying your truth even in managing wealth that you may be glorified in me! Bless me as I bless others! I ask this in Jesus's name! Amen.

LIFE LESSONS

In this chapter, I will share our personal testimony in order for you to understand how Ann and I can relate to your debt crisis. Read closely as with this chapter we will start sharing the biblical truths and God given practical applications we learned through our financial crisis.

I'm excited about what God did and continues to do for Ann and me, and I know he will do the same for you if you put the principles and practical keys we share into practice.

I'm putting our personal experience in writing because I desire for you to experience the power of God in your lives! I desire for you to get excited about the mighty God, the creator of the universe, who cares about you and me!

Also, my desire is that by sharing what God has shown Ann and me, you, too, will be set free from spiritual and financial bondage so you can be a living testimony of God's grace, mercy, and power to those you associate with in your life!

Our prayer is that when others see what God has done for you, they will have a desire to know this God you serve.

I remind you, God does not love Ann and me any more than he loves you—what he did for us he will also do for you!

At the tender age of thirteen, I accepted Jesus as my savior. Sadly, at the age of fifteen, I turned from God and led a very sinful life until I met my wife in 1970 and was wonderfully restored to a vital relationship with God shortly before we were married. Since that moment, I have passionately and faithfully sought to know him and serve him with all my soul, my mind, and my strength.

> And Jesus answered him, The first of all the commandments is, Hear, O Israel; The Lord our God is one Lord: And thou shalt love the Lord thy God with all thy heart, and

with all thy soul, and with all thy mind, and with all thy strength: this is the first commandment.

Mark 12:29–30 (KJV)

I give credit to my walk with God to my wonderful wife who insisted I attend church if I was going to date her and encouraged me to find a deep and lasting relationship with God. We met on August 19, 1970, and married on November 22 of the same year.

🗝 **I learned at a young age that when you see a good thing, grab it and hold on to it.**

I'm committed in whatever I do. I'm committed to my marriage, to the Lord, to the ministry, and to helping others to experience the peace and joy first of all in knowing and serving a mighty God as well as a life of debt-free living. God is my hope, my strength and my help. Likewise, he is your only hope, strength, and help during your financial crisis.

God has been faithful to Ann and me, supplying all of our needs according to his riches. To him is the glory!

Since returning to the Lord, I have been faithful to him serving my local church some forty plus years holding the positions of deacon, teacher, church treasurer, youth minister, trustee, chairman of administration/stewardship committee, a missionary to Peru, and as a stewardship minister. As stewardship minister, I counseled and assisted individuals with developing and maintaining budgets. I became a mediator for those I counseled with their creditors and providers of medical and social services. I assisted my senior pastor in administering the church's benevolence funds for the poor and needy and the mission funds. However, in 2011, we felt called to expand our teaching and counseling ministry beyond my local church, and thus, we birthed Life Ministries as an independent ministry.

It is our mission to empower you with the truth of God's word that will set you free from spiritual and financial bondage and give you the ability to empower your local church through a renewed lifestyle of debt-free living to effectively minister in all areas of ministry to the laity and to a lost and dying world.

I was born in Jacksonville, North Carolina, and raised with my two younger brothers mainly in the small rural farming communities around Richlands and Back Swamp in Onslow County, North Carolina. My father and mother worked a farm to provide a living until I was about three years old. My dad determined that farming did not provide adequate income to support our family, so he took a position as an auto mechanic. Dad continued this trade until he had a stroke at the age of seventy. He was never able to return to the work force after the stroke and died a few months after his eightieth birthday.

When my younger brother and I were in elementary school, my mother took a position as a waitress to provide additional income. Sadly, my mom and dad divorced a few years later after my youngest brother was born. This was one of the most traumatic experiences in my life! Thankfully, neither parent ever tried to turn my brothers or me against the other parent. This is a big mistake many parents make during a divorce. Out of anger, divorced spouses sometimes will use the children to inflict pain to the other spouse. This is wrong. Children are already dealing with their own anger and the feelings of rejection and abandonment. Regardless of the reason for a divorce and the existing tension between the parents, children deeply love Mom and Dad, and they need the love, affection and guidance of both Mom and Dad. It is spiritually, emotionally, and physically wrong to deprive a child of experiencing love from either parent.

Because neither of my parents talked about what led up to their divorce, I was in my late forties before I learned of their reasoning. Although as a child this created many questions, I later understood that not knowing actually was for my best interest so I could have a good relationship with both parents. At the time of their divorce, Mom and Dad decided my three brothers and I would remain with our dad. After the divorce, mom continued to see my brothers and me when she could and send gifts for special occasions. As a child, I really missed having a mom at home. As an adult, I miss having the family portraits of a complete family.

However, because of the divorce, I became a very angry young man during my teen years! Only God was able to heal the anger, the feelings of abandonment, and associated hurt and pain I experienced from the divorce and gave me the ability for forgiveness at the age of twenty. If you are the child of divorced parents, God can and will give you healing and give you the ability to forgive so you can find peace and restoration if you will turn to him and develop a deep and intimate relationship with him.

Today, I have a wonderful and loving relationship with my mother. I cherish the times we spend together. I'm thankful that although my mom and dad divorced, later, they were friends making it easier on my brothers and me to have a relationship with both of them.

During my growing up years, Dad did the best he could to provide for us often working on cars after getting off from his regular job. Dad was a very hardworking man, but he made very little money so we were financially poor. However, I didn't know we were poor because everyone we knew was also financially poor. Although we had very little money, my father made sure we did not go hungry and we had a home to live in. We grew a lot of our food so we never received food stamps or welfare. Money was really tight and because Dad worked two jobs, often we would only see him at breakfast and on Sundays unless we stayed up past our bed time. Dad was under a lot of stress so at the age of fifteen, it was mutually decided between my brothers, Dad, and me that we would go to an orphanage until Dad could get out from under his debt bondage. Apparently, he had never recovered from debts during the years he was a farmer, and they just continued to compound trying to raise three boys. I learned years after I graduated from high school and married that my

Dad paid off his last remaining farming debt when I graduated. He was excited because he was debt-free. The monkey was off his back!

Dad believed if you owed a man, you must pay him even if it took years to accomplish. Somewhere, people have lost this concept of paying their debt. Bankruptcy has become the leading tool used to break a contract which is breaking your word to repay debts. This is wrong, and I will speak more on this in later chapters.

Today, I have framed in my office a front auto plate from Dad's old mercury that says, "I Owe, I Owe, So Off to Work I Go." Debt bondage is a miserable life to live! I saw it beat a good man down and then continue to beat him all of his life. Since then I have counseled and seen so many families broken to pieces by debt with seemly no hope of ever finding restoration. Is this really the life you desire? It doesn't have to be your life story. Debt bondage was the life Dad knew and the life I knew before God showed me how to get out of debt.

Warning: This will most likely be the life your children will know if you live a life of debt unless you turn to God and turn your life around to living within your means. You can experience peace and joy in your life and pass the experience down to your children but only if you will seek God for a relationship and seek his wisdom while applying the principles and practical keys in this book.

Throughout this book, I will use the word *wealth*, but my intent does not necessarily always agree with the common thought of having a lot of money. In my opinion, real wealth is not necessarily measured by money.

🔑 **Real wealth is anything God has entrusted unto us whether it is money, property, or family. Real wealth is also good friends that will stand by you and will tell you truth even**

if it causes pain to help you develop your character. Real wealth can even be your personal integrity.

My family may have been poor financially, but we were rich in so many other areas of our lives. For that, I'm grateful. I believe these things helped to lay a foundation for my character development.

I learned a lot of good lessons from my dad. I remember one day my dad was telling me that the greatest possession I had was my word. "You don't own your cars or your house. If you don't believe me, just fail to pay the taxes, and you will see the government owns them so you don't own anything but your word." He said, "Above all things, let your word be your word."

> But let your communication be, Yea, yea; Nay, nay: for whatsoever is more than these cometh of evil.
>
> Matthew 5:37 (KJV)

My father taught me to be honest, to pay men what you owe them no matter how long it takes, to work hard, to give people more than they expect, and to always treat people with respect, especially elders, and to help others when you can.

> Owe no man any thing, but to love one another: for he that loveth another hath fulfilled the law.
>
> Romans 13:8 (KJV)

Jesus said the following:

> And the King shall answer and say unto them, Verily I say unto you, Inasmuch as ye have done it unto one of the least of these my brethren, ye have done it unto me.
>
> Matthew 25:40 (KJV)

The older I get, the more I understand just how wise my father was. He laid a good foundation that helps me stand in my faith with God today!

Often, men marvel and esteem men of great wealth and credit them with having great wisdom without even knowing how they accumulated the wealth. I've know some very wise men that were not wealthy. I'm sure there are rich men that lack real wisdom. My opinion is this: wisdom is not measured by wealth.

🗝 **Wisdom is measured by the daily application of God's received truth!**

A wise man will receive and apply God's word consistently throughout his life. A wise man will walk in the Spirit and not in the flesh! You can use the wisdom I share in this book to get you out of debt, but unless you apply this wisdom consistently for the rest of your life, you will not be wise.

Another lesson I learned at an early age from my dad is this:

🗝 **Nothing is really free; we should work to gain and provide for our family.**

Have you ever had someone to give you something and later ask a favor of you? You then felt obligated to grant their request because they did you a favor. There are individuals that once they give you something, you always owe them. No matter how much you do for them, they constantly ask for more. I see the same situations for birthdays, weddings, and baby showers whether it is family, friends, or just somebody who is an acquaintance. Once you receive a gift, you feel obligated to give gifts at special events in their life. It becomes a never-ending cycle! So are gifts really free?

There are a lot of people that constantly look for a free handout from any source they can get it. This is a major problem in our economy today! Because of this mindset of getting something for nothing, politicians have promoted and created all kinds of social programs that have greatly contributed to the national debt, higher taxes for working people, and these social programs encourages people not to work. In fact, many of these programs penalize people from securing part-time jobs or securing jobs paying far less wages than the average household can survive on to meet basic household expenses. The recipients of the social programs then stay at home and sign up for more programs and have more children because this will increase their benefits. These programs are not free. They are costing the working people. Politicians know these facts yet they will not dare suggest dropping or redesigning the social programs because it will cost them reelection. But God's word gives clear instructions concerning laziness!

> For even when we were with you, this we commanded you, that if any would not work, neither should he eat.
>
> 2 Thessolianians 3:10 (KJV)

I have met people who took the teachings of Jesus in Matthew 6:19–34 out of context and used it for an excuse not to work. Apparently, in Paul's day, there were those that were lazy and were looking to the church to support them just as they are today. Churches and charitable organizations are bombarded by free loaders unwilling to work. They go from church to church and charities looking for a handout. Don't misunderstand me as there are legitimate situations where people are needy and poor and need assistance, but God has given guidance in his written word for you, your church, and me on how to distribute what he entrust unto us.

God's word is clear that we are to help the poor and needy, but who is really poor and who is needy? I wrestled with these terms when I first started counseling though I have developed an understanding through my years of counseling when it comes to assisting.

Poor is a continual financial position while needy is a temporary position. Perhaps, a needy person has been a good steward, but because of a loss of job or catastrophic medical bills they could not possibly prepare for, they need assistance.

There are people who are poor or needy because they are lazy, or consistently use bad judgment, or become addicted to various substances such as illegal drugs, alcohol, tobacco, etc. Then there are people who are poor or needy through no fault of their own. They are not able or they are barely able to meet their basic, frugal needs of food, clothing, shelter, medical care and cannot provide for life's large financial circumstances that are going to happen.

Likewise, there are people who are considered needy through no fault of their own because they are not able to temporarily meet their basic, frugal needs of food, clothing, shelter, medical care, or some life circumstance that financially they could not possibly have foreseen. An example might be a situation where they lost their job or had a major illness that had catastrophic, financial expenses.

Paul gave strict guidance to the church leadership to let a lazy man go hungry. The intent for the creation of the government welfare system was good for those that are disabled, abandoned, and truly cannot work to provide for themselves and their children. But it is drastically abused and has become a stumbling block encouraging laziness. In America today, the government welfare program has replaced the obligation of the extended family and the church to discern the situation and give financial or other support in alignment with God's word. Churches need to review the Scriptures, find the heart of God, and then put into practice what the word truly declares. If this would happen, churches would see more of God's blessings, and there would be no need for government welfare programs. My local church returned to these scriptural mandates and guidelines several years ago. The results were God blessed with more money than we gave out in assistance. We learned the keys that are essential to successfully distribute God's money to help others.

🔑 **Always listen for God to speak! Short of hearing directly from God in a situation: Help the poor and needy who, through no fault of their own, need assistance and those who have demonstrated true repentance.**

In counseling I have encountered situations where I did not get immediate confirmation in my spirit as to what I was supposed to do. In these circumstances, I defaulted to the Scriptures as my guide. The Scriptures are plain that we are to help the poor and needy, so I would give them the financial assistance they needed. Sometimes, this was okay, but at other times, I honestly have missed what God was trying to do in the life of the individuals. My heart was right in giving the financial assistance, and so I believe God forgave my interference in his work. But God desires us to learn from every situation so as not to continue making bad decisions. Therefore, it is important that you:

🔑 **Discern what God is doing in the life of the individual at that moment, and discern if God desires you to assist and how to assist.**

I have learned not to be hasty in making decisions, thus allowing God time to give discernment. Knowledge is powerful. I normally ask questions about the person's spiritual condition, what led to the crisis, and about their lifestyle. I find in many situations through asking questions, I gain knowledge that allows the Holy Spirit to speak discernment into my spirit.

Let me warn that financial assistance is not always the answer. Often, God's direction is counsel. Far too many churches have left the biblical principles concerning discernment and distribution. Church leadership and committees have developed and implemented a simple benevolence plan to appease their hearts for failing to administer assistance according to God's heart and the guidelines given in his word. Often, this simple plan is to give everyone that comes into the door asking for assistance a set amount of $25 or maybe $50. This is an easy plan because the leadership doesn't have to say no, the leadership doesn't have to seek discernment. Giving a fixed amount that is less than the need is not the help they need! When the individual needs $150 to keep the power company from turning off the power and they only receive $50, more than likely their power is going to be turned off unless they go from one charity or church to another and the accumulation equals the need. But now they may have created a need for gas money or grocery money because they used what little money they had to purchase gas. Don't get me wrong. I'm not saying the church should pay every bill. What I am saying is that the leadership of the church needs to find discernment in each situation to know what God desires them to do. God may say pay the bill or he may say no, I'm dealing with this individual to draw his or her heart to me, and this is the moment to give spiritual counsel for repentance, commitment, and obedience to God's word.

A lot of churches don't have benevolence ministry funds so the leadership either has to dig from their own pockets or just simply tell the individuals "I'm sorry, but our church doesn't have funds for benevolence." I would challenge any ministry, board of deacons and/or ministers to go back to the scriptures and find God's heart in this matter of helping the poor and needy. I'm not saying operating a benevolence ministry is easy. I am saying that any church that is not in alignment with God's heart and his written word is missing God's blessings.

Although, I have spoken a lot about benevolence ministry in regard to the church and charitable ministries, this still does not release the individual from their personal obligation to help the poor and needy. Likewise, these same given principles found in God's word apply for you in distributing the money God has entrusted to you.

God has given a divine order for seeking and receiving assistance.

🔑 Assistance for the poor and needy should first come from their blood family.

Not only are we required by God to work and provide for our immediate family, but the commandment also applies to our extended family. This includes aunts, uncles, cousins, grandparents, and parents.

> But if any provide not for his own, and specially for those of his own house, he hath denied the faith, and is worse than an infidel.
>
> 1 Timothy 5:8 (KJV)

These are some strong words that should not be taken lightly. God requires us to assist our blood relatives in alignment with biblical guidelines. Again, if they are just lazy, then there is no requirement to assist unless there is true recognizable repentance.

🔑 The second source of assistance for the poor and needy is their church family or their church.

The church or some charitable organization appears to be the first place people run to when they have a financial need. But, according to God's word, the blood family has the first responsibility to assist. Where there is no blood family or the blood family really does not have the means to help, then and only then should an individual come to their church or church family for assistance, and then the church should administer assistance according to discernment and God's guidelines. I use the terms church and church family to give a distinction of how a financial need is met. Although every church should have a benevolence fund, there are times when God has financially prepared individuals within a church to provide the needed financial assistance for a particular situation. Supplying the financial needs for the poor and needy should never be restricted to the boundaries of a church fund. By wisdom and discernment for some situations, the leadership should approach the family of God and let them know the need, allowing the Holy Spirit to speak to individuals within the congregation, thus allowing the congregation to receive a blessing for their sacrifice and obedience in assisting another person. Except in rare situations, my local church leadership only informs the congregation of a special need within the congregation not mentioning the name of the individuals in need. The congregation respects the leaderships decision not to give a name, knowing the leadership would only bring before them a need they feel God desires the involvement of the church family. The practice of not announcing names does not add to the great humility of the individuals needing assistance. Having the ability to turn to your church and your church family in times of crises is a great benefit of being a Christian. I struggle with people whose only contact with churches is when there is a need for financial assistance.

I know it seems I took a detour from the application key to work for gain, but I felt it necessary to promote that God has given some requirements and guidelines not only to the church but to you in who and how to help. When I first got saved, anyone holding out a hand received financial assistance from me if I had a dollar in my pocket, and some of those took that money right to the store and bought liquor or tobacco products instead of buying food or paying their rent. You see individuals sitting beside the road with handmade signs saying "will work for money or food." Put them to the test. Offer them some work and listen to their response. It will not take long to discern if they are legitimate and have a desire to work.

My brothers and I learned to work for what we got. Dad and Mom never gave us an allowance! We had daily chores that had to be performed without financial compensation. Our compensation was a roof over our heads, a bed to sleep in, food to eat, and clothes to wear.

Although I will not say allowances are wrong, I do wonder if allowances don't instill a sense of entitlement in children and encourages laziness. "You are my parents and you are supposed to give to me!" I've seen children always expecting something for nothing rather than learning to work for gain. I wonder how their marriages will work. Most employers will tell you today that most people they hire want a pay check without giving the adequate labor to justify the check. When was this instilled in their minds?

My brothers and I did earn money for work beyond our normal chores. Even before I was old enough to go to school, I remember pulling weeds around the tree roots at our home and Dad giving my younger brother and me money for the work we did. He didn't give us the same amount. He gave according to our accomplishment. Today, we don't want to hurt feelings so we reward every child whether they deserve a reward or not. What we are teaching today's children is just show up, give little effort, and still be rewarded. We are killing the challenge to exceed and the incentive for going beyond. I have seen the spirit of good men broken that gave their all in the work place, because no matter how much they did, the guy that did very little received the same compensation at the end of the week. This mindset of reward all is broken! You will not ruin the self-esteem of a child because he or she did not get a reward or equal reward for failing to apply him or herself. Rather, it is a teachable moment that with love, you can share truth that encourages them to strive for excellence in all they do for the rest of their lives.

Beginning at the age of six, during the summer, I earned money working with my grandfather on his farm. Later, I worked with my uncles and with other farmers until I was seventeen and accepted a job in the retail business. I suppose the money I earned during the early years of my childhood helped purchase my school clothes because it left my hands and went to my parent's hands, and I didn't see it again. I do know that in my teen years, I earned my spending money and bought most of my school clothes and made my car payments. I believe this was all good for me as I learned to appreciate the things I do have and to work hard, giving my employers something above a fair day's work for a fair day's wages.

Sadly, one of the most important lessons I did not learn from my parents was how to live within my means! This would have saved Ann, our children, and me a lot of suffering and stress in the earlier years.

> But godliness with contentment is great gain.
>
> 1 Timothy 6:6 (KJV)

As far as I know, after the farming experience with the exception of buying a mobile home and then a house, my dad never again made it a practice to borrow money. He tried to live within his meager means! To this day, my mother lives within her means in her retirement practices. I am so proud of her! Yes, there are financial situations beyond her control, and God requires her children to assist with those. But for her basic needs, she lives within her means.

Parents, it is your responsibility to teach your children this very important principle of money management.

🔑 Live within your income!

Your lifestyle is the most effective teaching tool you have. It is hypocritical to tell your kids not to do something you are doing!

You have heard it said, "A picture is worth a thousand words."

🔑 Your lifestyle is the picture your children see, and it will influence their life patterns!

The school system teaches a lot of good subjects, but your children are not going to learn at school how to reconcile their bank statement with their check register or how to develop and live within a budget. I didn't learn these lessons, and it cost me dearly. Thank God I was rescued from this path of self-destruction!

A life of poor financial management finally caught up with me. I was working in a good job paying above average wages, but I was not living within my means. Years earlier, I had based my standard of living upon overtime. When the overtime stopped in 1981, my accumulated debts didn't, so I got deeper in debt. I had maxed out five credit cards, and I had just purchased a new house when the overtime stopped. I had ignored the red flag that arose when my base salary was not enough to borrow the money to buy the home. I had to get a statement from my supervisor telling how much overtime I normally worked to be able to secure the loan. This was a big mistake.

🔑 **Pay attention to the red flags God puts in front of you to help you make decisions.**

When the overtime stopped, it reduced my annual income considerably. I couldn't figure out how I was paying all my debt and could not seem to get anything paid off to give me some financial relief. Our financial situation was so bad that even family members told me I should file bankruptcy. But my dad had taught me to pay my bills somehow. So I walked the roads and picked up aluminum cans to sell to buy gas to go to work. I worked two or more jobs in a day cutting pulp wood, bagging groceries, or doing carpentry and other construction work just to survive. Because I could not afford to lose one hours pay, I went to work when I was too sick to work; sometimes, I was on so much medication that I could not think straight. This was dangerous as my job consisted of working on large lathes and cutting machines and often running a chain saw. However, I had no choice as I was a slave to debt and my creditors!

In 1986 when I thought things could not get any worst, my supervisor called a meeting at the end of the shift. And then the final blow came, I was laid off of my job of twelve years. This really caught me by surprise. I had no money in the bank and didn't know what to do.

Even before my layoff, our situation got so bad it became a sacrifice for me to give a dollar in the offering plate. Yes, I paid my tithes, but let me tell you that when you violate other principles in God's word, tithing alone will not reverse the fact you are going to reap what you have sown.

I came home that day, sat down on my couch with a knot in my stomach, and cried before the Lord. I knew I had made a lot of bad financial decisions, and now it had caught up with me. I knew we were going to lose everything we had accumulated, and I had no idea of what I was going to do. I had failed my family. I had failed God. Believe me, I know what it means to reap what you sow. However, I knew God had been merciful to me and my family over the years and right there on my couch, I began to praise God for his mercy and for allowing me to work twelve years in a good paying job. At that point, I moved from a spirit of despair to a spirit of worship!

> 🔑 **We must have a heart of gratefulness for God's faithfulness and what he provided in our past and for what he is going to provide in the present and the future.**

I believe gratefulness is a key for us to go through any crisis in our life!

It was hard for me to tell my wife I had lost my job. I didn't know what we were going to do. However, the next day I received a phone call from the personnel department telling me that because of a technical point in the employee handbook, I had the opportunity to downgrade to a previous position I held at a lesser pay if I wanted it. Hey, I was going to lose everything! Of course I would accept the job! I returned to work the following day missing only one day of work! That was God's mercy! At that point, I knew God had once again been merciful and was giving me a second chance. Somehow, I knew I had to get out of debt. But I really didn't know what to do. I had tried for the previous five years without success.

God was working to change my mindset and my financial situation. While I was trying to find discernment and inspiration for my financial needs, my pastor was trying to find discernment and inspiration for the local church. On a Sunday morning, he announced to the church that God had called him on a twenty-one-day fast for the church and invited those that desired to join him to fast some meals or days during this twenty-one-day period. After the morning service, I felt God calling me to join him in this fast. Understand that I had missed a meal once in a while, but I had never fasted a whole day much less twenty-one days. This was quite a commitment, but I felt this conviction, and I was desperate to hear from God, not only for my church but especially for my financial situation. I will not go into details of fasting in this book but only say this was a God-called fast! Listen to me, you can't fast twenty-one days while working a physically, labor-intensive job unless it is God called! In fact, I would not recommend a fast beyond three days unless it is a God-called fast. Through this fast, I learned some valuable lessons. Keys that redeveloped my mindset and deepened my relationship with God. Since I had never fasted before, I drank nothing and I ate nothing the first week. My wise pastor saw my weakness and gave me godly advice to drink some water throughout the fast. He also counseled me on what to expect during the fast. I remember him telling me that after a period of time in the fast, the devil would speak to me and tell me God was pleased with me, that I had done well and that I could come off the fast. After a couple of weeks into the fast, it happened just like he said. I immediately rebuked the devil and began to praise God for his mercy. During the fast, I would become very weak, so during my lunch break, I would get alone and read the Bible and pray. Amazingly, I would rise up from my break, refreshed and strengthened like I had eaten a good meal. My Pastor also instructed me that in a God-called fast, you will be hungry the first few days then the hunger would leave, but it would return again when the fast was over. This was excellent advice as in future fasts I didn't set time limits; I just waited until the hunger returned. I later understood my pastor was the most fasting and praying man I had ever known, and more importantly, was a man God constantly speaks to.

> **To develop good habits and a heart that hears from God, find a godly man to fellowship with and follow his godly habits.**

We have an example of this mentoring in the Old Testament (I Kings 19; 2 Kings 2) with Elijah and Elisha and in the New Testament book of Acts with Paul and Timothy and the other apostles and disciples. You see godly men training godly men in the ways of God through their lifestyle. I recommend you find a godly man or woman and follow after his or her good habits. I warn you, don't put your faith in men as your faith is only reserved toward God. Men can fail you, but God never fails. Another important lesson I learned about fasting that you should also learn.

> **Fasting is not to give you some special power, but humbles your spirit so that you can hear God speaking.**

Because of my financial situation like anyone else that is in debt, I thought I needed more money to resolve my financial dilemma. The first seventeen days of the fast, I asked God to give me more money so I could get out of debt. However, this was not working. Was God hearing my prayers?

> Ye ask, and receive not, because ye ask amiss, that ye may consume it upon your lusts.
>
> James 4:3 (KJV)

Earlier, I told you that God has a plan for any wealth he entrust into your care. Why would he entrust more unto you if you are a poor steward of what you have now?

> He that is faithful in that which is least is faithful also in much: and he that is unjust in the least is unjust also in much. If therefore ye have not been faithful in the unrighteous mammon, who will commit to your trust the true riches? And if ye have not been faithful in that which is another man's, who shall give you that which is your own? No servant can serve two masters: for either he will hate the one, and love the other; or else he will hold to the one, and despise the other. Ye cannot serve God and mammon.
>
> Luke 16:10–13 (KJV)

Thankfully, the Holy Spirit pointed this truth out to me, and I stopped asking God for more money and started asking God to give me wisdom to wisely use the money I was making. I promised him I would do whatever he told me. This was a transformation of my mind and my spirit from secular thinking to spiritual thinking. God says,

> Seek ye the LORD while he may be found, call ye upon him while he is near: Let the wicked forsake his way, and the unrighteous man his thoughts: and let him return unto the LORD, and he will have mercy upon him; and to our God, for he will abundantly pardon.For my thoughts are not your thoughts, neither are your ways my ways, saith the LORD. For as the heavens are higher than the earth, so are my ways higher than your ways, and my thoughts than your thoughts. For as the rain cometh down, and the snow from heaven, and returneth not thither, but watereth the earth,

and maketh it bring forth and bud, that it may give seed to the sower, and bread to the eater: So shall my word be that goeth forth out of my mouth: it shall not return unto me void, but it shall accomplish that which I please, and it shall prosper in the thing whereto I sent it. For ye shall go out with joy, and be led forth with peace: the mountains and the hills shall break forth before you into singing, and all the trees of the field shall clap their hands.

Isaiah 55:6–12 (KJV)

Let me tell you, when God gives you a word, it does not depart from your inner being! When you apply his word, it brings life, it brings fulfillment, it brings joy not only to you but to all those around you. Your spirit changes, your mind changes, your heart changes, your ways change. I began to immediately change my spending habits and became extremely frugal. My wife said I became tight with money.

I didn't end my request for wisdom with my weekly income. I also told God if he did allow me additional money, I would first pay my tithe and the remaining 90 percent I would use to pay off debt. Later God tested me on this promise, and joyfully, I complied and passed the test.

🔑 **Seek God's wisdom that is greater than man's wisdom for God desires to impart his wisdom unto you.**

> If any of you lack wisdom, let him ask of God, that giveth to all men liberally, and upbraideth not; and it shall be given him.
>
> James 1:5 (KJV)

I would love to share a day by day walk of what transpired after this transformation. However, that would require a book in itself. I can say from that point on there were many miraculous interventions by God in my life, and he continued to pour wisdom into my mind concerning our financial situation.

Remember, I had told God if he allowed additional money, I would apply it toward debt. Well, I was sitting in church on a Sunday night after I had made this commitment to God. The pastor was receiving the offering and asked the congregation to pray and ask God what to give. As I was praying, God spoke to me and told me to give $5.

> My sheep hear my voice, and I know them, and they follow me:
>
> John 10:27 (KJV)

I was so deeply in debt, but I made sure I paid my tithes; however, it was a great sacrifice to give even $1 in offering. Now God is asking me to give $5. I knew I had taken $5 out of my pay for the next week's expenses. I reached into my pocket and opened my wallet to pull out the money, but there was not $5 in it! I forgot I had stopped and got $2 worth of gas on the way to church. Right there in church, the devil laughed at me. It was just as real as any human standing beside me. Yes! Satan comes to church! He causes division, strife, and discontentment among the membership and congregation. He said, "Ha-ha-ha! You thought it was God that told you to give $5? And you didn't even have $5!" You see, Satan desires to sow doubt in your mind that you can hear God speak! But I knew God's voice. I immediately looked over to my wife and asked her if she had the check book. We had quit bringing the check book to church because I was subject to give on impulse that which we could not afford! Let me say this, good Christians.

🔑 God will never ask you to give that which you don't have or that which he will not miraculously supply!

Remember when Peter was confronted and asked if Jesus paid taxes? Peter's response was yes! It is apparent from the Scriptures that Peter didn't have any money. Peter went to inquire of Jesus.

Jesus's response was that the tax should be paid! He gave Peter the instructions to secure the money, but it required Peter to move on faith.

🔑 **God may require you to do something beyond natural reasoning in order to show you his power and mercy.**

> Notwithstanding, lest we should offend them, go thou to the sea, and cast an hook, and take up the fish that first cometh up; and when thou hast opened his mouth, thou shalt find a piece of money: that take, and give unto them for me and thee.
>
> Matthew 17:27 (KJV)

This was God's miraculous intervention! God intervened for me, and he will do the same for you if you will respond according to his instructions.

🔑 **When God says give, he will provide!**

I can tell you, churches get bad checks all the time, because on impulse, someone will write a check when there was no money to cover. You must hear from God before you give what you don't have!

Getting back to our testimony, my wife looked at me puzzled and said, "Yes, I have the check book." I told her to write a five-dollar check for the offering. She said, "You want me to write a check for five dollars?" She knew our financial situation, but being submissive, she wrote the check! I knew I had five dollars in the bank to cover the check, but I also knew we would have to sacrifice something the next week to give the five dollars!

Here is an example of how God provides when he tells you to give. Monday morning, the first-shift supervisor called me and told me the first shift operator was out and he needed me to come in early. It had been about a year since I had received any overtime! That was God's grace in my faithfulness to hear him and respond correctly of his word to sacrifice. That five dollar offering was multiplied ten times! The next Sunday night, our pastor told us again to pray and ask God what to give. I prayed, and God told me to give $10. I immediately opened my wallet and responded. (Note: the devil didn't laugh this time!) Monday morning, I got another phone call from the first shift supervisor. He told me the first shift operator was sick and would be out all week, and he asked me to come in early all week. That ten dollar offering was multiplied fifty times!

Believe me, I was rejoicing! I continued to pray every Sunday for a long time, asking God what he wanted me to give, but I didn't always hear an exact amount as before. I have learned the lessons God desired, and so it is not necessary for him to give me an exact amount every week. There are still times that I feel a special unction of the Holy Spirit to ask or to give a specific amount. I don't work overtime every time I respond, but it is amazing how God gives me additional funds when I respond correctly. I am faithful to administer these extra funds as I had promised, and God is faithful to provide.

On another occasion, the church was raising money for missions and was asking for pledges. Most of the members stood up and were pledging $100. Again, I prayed. I felt compelled of the Spirit to pledge $10. I had learned to trust God. I know this is a small amount, but I didn't have $10 to give. Remember, I was putting any additional money on debts minus my tithe. However, I knew I could pick up enough aluminum cans to raise $10. The next week, I was walking down the road picking up cans. I had travelled about a mile when I spotted something green that was different from the grass in the median. I crossed the road to see what was so different, and there lay a $10 bill. I began to praise God for his faithfulness. Now, I could have praised the Lord and went back home, but I continued to pick up cans earning more than the pledge. This is the God I serve! There were many events similar to these that have continued through the years. Again, I say what God did for Ann and me, he will do for you!

🔑 God continually blesses when we are faithful to hear and respond correctly!

> But be ye doers of the word, and not hearers only, deceiving your own selves. For if any be a hearer of the word, and not a doer, he is like unto a man beholding his natural face in a glass: For he beholdeth himself, and goeth his way, and straightway forgetteth what manner of man he was. But whoso looketh into the perfect law of liberty, and continueth therein, he being not a forgetful hearer, but a doer of the work, this man shall be blessed in his deed.
>
> James 1:22–25 (KJV)

I will tell you that in my wisdom, we could not get out of debt. We had tried for five years! But God gave me the wisdom we needed, and fourteen months later, we had paid off every debt except our mortgage. Applying this same wisdom, six and a half years later, we paid off a twenty-year mortgage. I can't describe in words the burden that lifted from me as I arose the next morning after paying off the mortgage. Before, when I was in bondage to debt, I could not afford to miss one hour of work. I can't tell you how many times I went to work though I was too sick because I had no other choice, but that next morning, I arose and realized that if I was sick, I could stay home. To God be the Glory!

🔑 Hear the wisdom of God and apply it faithfully the rest of your life, and you will not be in financial bondage!

Why can I say this? First, I can say this because God is *faithful*! Second, I can say this because you will learn and practice living within your means! Wow, what a concept it is to actually only spend within the limits of what you make! This concept has been lost in our generation. We bitterly complain about our governments spending habits yet our government is a reflection of the general population's habits. We want everything, and we want it now so we borrow to get it. I can tell you that borrowing has driven up the cost of consumer goods.

What would our economy look like if everyone practiced living within their means? It sure would change the face of the business world! For one thing, payday loan companies and consolidation debt companies would have to close their doors. Living within our means would drive down the cost of goods and services as the demand decreased. Consumers would not be paying hundreds of thousands of dollars in interest in their lifetime. What would you do if you had one hundred thousand dollars extra to spend?

When I became a missionary to Peru right after the 2008 earthquake, this concept of living within your means became even more a reality to me. The families I ministered to had nothing before the earthquake. Most families made less than $150 a month yet they were living! You might say, well, the cost of living in Peru is cheaper. But I can tell you, when I went to the stores in Peru, most prices were comparable to the prices in the United States. Where I did see savings was in labor and medical cost. I understand in any third world country the same can be said.

The fact remains, you can live within your income! People did it during the depression in the United States! It takes commitment and assistance.

> I can do all things through Christ which strengtheneth me.
>
> Philippians 4:13 (KJV)

I will continue to remind you, God does not love my wife or me any more than he loves you. What he did for us, he will do for you! You may be feeling like there is no hope for your situation, but my God, the one and only God, is your hope! You may be head over heels in debt, and you don't know what to do. I can tell you from experience that you do not have the wisdom to fix your problem.

🔑 God has the Wisdom, and he will give it to you if you ask.

Remember,

> If any of you lack wisdom, let him ask of God, that giveth to all men liberally, and upbraideth not; and it shall be given him.
>
> James 1:5 (KJV)

God speaks his wisdom to men in many ways, and I am only one of his messengers. Since 1986, I have been sharing with others what God gave to me and have seen God do the same thing for those willing to obey. Sadly, I have also seen too many reject the wisdom and remain in bondage.

My life has never been the same since I heard God speak, and I responded according to his instructions. He has continued to speak to me for my personal situations, my children, and to give directions to my local church. His blessings to me, to my children, and to my church are innumerable. He can do the same for you!

I am not trying to force you into doing anything against your will. God gives you the liberty to choose life or death, and he also gives you the liberty to live in bondage or to be free! It's your choice! I pray you will choose to be free.

In the next chapter, we will share more keys to understanding God's plan for your life and how to become debt-free.

Pray this prayer before proceeding to the next chapter,

> Father, you gave me the Scriptures that I might learn your will and your ways! Open my eyes that I might see! Open my ears that I might hear! Let me hear your voice! Give me grace to change my ways and to experience your power

in my life. I commit from this day forward to walk in the light of your word and in your Holy Spirit that my life might inspire others to seek and glorify your name. In Jesus's name, I ask these things. Amen.

GET OUT OF DEBT: GOD'S PLAN

We give very little thought to using credit to purchase what we want, but I have read the average person owes at least $8,000 on their credit cards and more than $150,000 in other loans. Borrowing to obtain is the norm in our society. We borrow to buy new cars, houses, furniture, recreational equipment, and electronic gadgets. But have you noticed that uneasy feeling in your gut when you sign a note for a significant sum of money? You will question yourself, "Did I do the right thing?" I believe God put an indicator in our inner being that alerts us that.

🔑 **Debt and bondage is not God's plan!**

The Exodus of the Israelites from Egypt to the entering in of the promise land is symbolic of bondage to freedom. God desires to deliver his children from bondage and give his children freedom. We will continue to remind you throughout this book that you can be set free from spiritual and debt bondage. Freedom doesn't mean life will always be easy! You can and will experience difficult times on your journey to freedom. We see in the Old Testament how life was hard on the wilderness journey and even when the children of Israel entered the promise land, there were many battles to fight. However, God was with them—and he is with you today! Because the Israelites were not completely obedient to God's word, they are still fighting battles. We should learn from history whatever God says, we are to do it precisely the way he says. You and I are on our journey to a promise land, but we have a much greater promise in eternity. We are to look forward to the end of our journey and not the present suffering to be successful. Don't be like the Israelites! On their journey, they began to complain and look back toward Egypt. They lost sight of their freedom and the bondage under their task masters in Egypt. Ultimately, it cost them their lives and the promise land (which would have represented total freedom if only they had been consistent to obey God's word). The Israelites knew the story of Lot's wife who looked back leaving Sodom and Gomorrah and it cost her life. Yet, they did not learn the lesson being taught. You cannot afford to look back once you start your journey to financial freedom. You have thrown the debt monkey off your back; keep him off! To achieve financial freedom, you must turn to God, receive and apply his word, and not look back! God's plan is not for you to be in bondage but to be free! Don't forget the bondage of your Egypt.

Learn this lesson well:

🔑 Borrowing causes you to become a slave!

> The rich ruleth over the poor, and the borrower is servant to the lender.
>
> Proverbs 22:7 (KJV)

If you don't believe borrowing causes you to be a slave then just don't go to work. Believe me, when the creditors start calling at all hours you will feel the stress. When you get hungry, you will feel the pain. When you lose your family, you will know the heartache. You are in bondage right where Satan desires for you to be! Debt is Satan's substitute for God's provisions! He will convince you that you deserve it, and debt is the way to obtain it. Remember, Satan's desire is to kill, steal, and destroy you! God's desire is to restore and bless you!

God's children need to understand.

🔑 God' plan for his people is to be a lender! He told Israel,

> For the LORD thy God blesseth thee, as he promised thee: and thou shalt lend unto many nations, but thou shalt not

borrow; and thou shalt reign over many nations, but they shall not reign over thee.

> Deuteronomy 15:6 (KJV)

God's blessings are dependent upon our obedience. Debt can surely be an indicator of a lack of obedience. You would need to read more in the Bible to fully understand God's plan of lending varies greatly from what you and I know today. Yes, lending was allowed in Old Testament days, but God made special provisions for lending to fellow brethren versus to the unbeliever. Lending to their brethren was without interest and had forgiveness periods. God desires to bless his people beyond their needs. I'm not teaching every Christian will be financially wealthy. Scriptures refutes the financial prosperity messages many ministers teach today for all Christians. Scriptures state there was and will always be poor people even among God's children that he desires for you to help.

> For the poor shall never cease out of the land: therefore I command thee, saying, Thou shalt open thine hand wide unto thy brother, to thy poor, and to thy needy, in thy land.
>
> Deuteronomy 15:11 (KJV)

God has a heart for the poor, and he is very serious about them not being mistreated or taken advantage of. He has given instructions to use our surplus for taking care of the needy and the poor.

> The wicked have drawn out the sword, and have bent their bow, to cast down the poor and needy, and to slay such as be of upright conversation. Their sword shall enter into their own heart, and their bows shall be broken.
>
> Psalm 37:14–15 (KJV)

God calls those who use their power to persecute the poor and needy wicked. Because God is the defender of the poor and needy, he will use the very instruments used by the wicked for their own destruction. In recent years we have seen this happen with wicked leaders in other nations. This is reaping what you sow. Rather than reaping destruction, God commands all men to:

> Defend the poor and fatherless: do justice to the afflicted and needy.
>
> Psalm 82:3 (KJV)

🔑 Provisions can indicate God's blessings!

I say provisions can indicate God's blessings because there are men with much provision that did not come from God. Satan also offers wealth! If Satan tried to use wealth to tempt Jesus, how much more does he use it to seduce and destroy men?

How do we know when God provides wealth versus Satan providing wealth? The answer is simple!

🔑 You know it is God's provisions when it is accompanied by peace.

> Peace I leave with you, my peace I give unto you: not as the world giveth, give I unto you. Let not your heart be troubled, neither let it be afraid.
>
> John 14:27 (KJV)

Wealth that comes through Satan is accompanied with worry, fear, continual greed, self-indulgence, even anger, and no peace. This is spiritual bondage!

God told the Israelites he would bless them, and they would be lenders if they followed his commandments. However, he also pronounced if they failed to follow his commandments, numerous curses would be evidenced.

🔑 Borrowing is a sign of a curse!

> He shall lend to thee, and thou shalt not lend to him: he shall be the head, and thou shalt be the tail. Moreover all these curses shall come upon thee, and shall pursue thee, and overtake thee, till thou be destroyed; because thou hearkenedst not unto the voice of the Lord thy God, to keep his commandments and his statutes which he commanded thee:
>
> Deuteronomy 28:44–45

I have not found anywhere in the scriptures where borrowing is forbidden, but all the Scriptures concerning borrowing have nothing good to say about it.

🔑 Borrowing is not God's best for you! He has a better plan, but it requires your obedience to his word!

If you are in debt, you are in bondage physically, mentally, and emotionally to the lender. Not only are you in bondage to the lender, you are in bondage to your employer because you must have that job to survive. Your spirit is in bondage. Your liberty to minister is in bondage. You are not free. You are shackled to that job, to that weekly paycheck. You must have it to survive. This is a miserable life!

I've seen some employers treat employees so badly and talk worst to them than they would to a dog. Sadly, I have been in this position. Because of my debt bondage, I couldn't afford to lose my job! Now that I'm free, I find I don't get so excited and upset anymore when seemingly I am being taken advantage of. Now, I ask myself this question, "Why am I here? God, what do you desire to teach me? What do you desire to teach others who associate with me? Do you desire me to influence my employer or those I work with toward good behavior and a change of heart with my humility?" Knowing that God has a purpose for where I am working at any given time gives me peace in my spirit. Paul found peace even in prison. One of the greatest changes I have experienced is now I can have peace in the midst of the storms of life. God has a purpose for all things. You also can experience this peace!

I know some of you are thinking we can't live without borrowing. To some degree, that may seem true in America. I see at least two reasons to support why people believe we can't live without borrowing:

> 🔑 **First: Many people have lost trust in God as the supplier of all our needs, forsaking his principles, and not living within their means.**

God has told us he will supply our needs, but many people have lost sight of needs versus wants and desires. Therefore, they seek to gain things their way, and thus, they come under debt bondage. Because they have left godly principles, many often fail to protect and provide properly for their children. Many people find themselves in a dilemma when all of a sudden they realize their child is old enough to go to college or even marry. They are not financially prepared for the cost involved in these major events. Because of little foresight and lack of planning, we fail and we often unintentionally set our children up for failure. I've counseled young men and women that were trying to start off life so heavy in debt with school loans it is nearly impossible for them to live. I have counseled other young couples that set up housekeeping in their new home, starting out with unrealistic, seemingly lifelong debts. I'm not saying every child needs to go to college as some are gifted for skilled trades like carpentry, cosmetology, welding, or electrical trades that can be learned through technical schools or apprentice programs. As parents, we must know our children and help guide them into the right life vocation. I know we agree it is not your heart for your children to be in debt bondage!

There must be a better way than debt to take care of our children's needs and for them to start out a life away from home. I believe God's word has the answers. Researching God's word gives principles not only for managing our finances today, but concerning inheritance as a possible means to provide for the education and marriage of our children rather than shackling them to debt.

Traditionally, we wait until we die to give all our inheritance to our children, but is this what we see being practiced in the Old and New Testament? Someone once said, "Don't wait to give me flowers at my death! Give them to me today that I might enjoy them." Could this be applied concerning inheritance? Why do we wait? Perhaps even investing a partial inheritance into education and assisting financially in helping our children to secure their own home would be more of a blessing to them than waiting until you die. Plus, you get to see the joy you bring into their lives.

Sadly, because of sticking to traditions and not practicing good stewardship, many parents can't or don't help their children's married lives get off to a good start. Oh, you might borrow to the hilt for that wedding day of your daughter, but she and your son-in-law starts life with nothing. Something seems very wrong when we spend thousands of dollars for a wedding but can't afford to help them set up housekeeping in a place of their own without them starting their new married life with the extreme pressures of debt. As a society, it has been instilled in our minds and we have instilled in our children pomp and ceremony beyond common sense. We justify extreme spending for one event over needs for the rest of their lives. Some balance needs to be brought to the table; otherwise, parents, unintentionally, are setting up children for failure!

It has been said that more than 50 percent of marriages fail, and more than 90 percent of those divorced say debt was the biggest contributor to arguments that contributed to the marriage failure. Could this have been avoided if parents had only properly planned financially to assist their children and properly trained their children in godly principles of stewardship?

I wish I had learned these lessons when my children were small because I failed to properly provide for and protect my own children. However, while alive, I am preparing to assist my children in providing and protecting my grandchildren for these life events.

Would it not be wise to begin financial preparation for college and marriage of your children today? Again, I believe God has addressed in his word principles to apply that will bless our children and give us peace of mind concerning our children's futures.

🗝 **Second: Easy financing has inflated prices on every product we need, so most people can't buy a home or car without borrowing.**

I told you earlier, my dad had a tag on the front of his car that said, "I owe, I owe, so off to work I go!" My youngest son framed that tag and it hangs on my office wall. I started out as a teen borrowing for a car, and it got easier and easier to borrow and the cars got bigger and bigger and more expensive until I learned better. I remember applying for my first credit card in the early seventies. I could only get a three hundred dollar limit card, and it was hard for me to obtain it! In those years, banks had a strict limit on what percentage of your monthly income could be used to get a loan or a credit card. Ironically, in the eighties when I was over my head in debt, I could get twelve- to fifteen-thousand-dollar-limit credit cards easily. Now credit card companies are bombarding college students to get their own card. Tell your children to run away from these offers as fast as they can. With the ease of credit, we buy what we really can't afford, and the demand for consumer goods continue to rise. Here we are in 2012, and all this easy credit is catching up with us. Foreclosures and bankruptcy are at an all time high. Banks and credit companies are closing due to over extending credit. Even our government outspends its income to the point our national debt is sixteen trillion dollars. Since World War II, we have been training each generation that credit is a good thing when God's word has nothing good to say about borrowing. Each generation has expanded upon this concept until we have driven the prices of houses, cars, and consumer goods to outrages prices.

I believe the greater damage of all this is that borrowing has ultimately forced most wives and moms to work public jobs to help provide for their families. Don't misunderstand me, ladies, it is not a sin for you to work a public job, and some of you have no choice. But I do not believe this is God's best for your family or for you if you have a spouse and children. Sadly, many wives and mothers must work public jobs to assist their husbands in supporting their lifestyle. But I believe wives working public jobs instead of remaining in the home to nurture and train their children and prepare a sanctuary of peace and love for their husbands to come home to may ultimately contribute to discipline problems with their children and marriage problems with their spouse. Because both parents work outside the home, now televisions, computers, and all-the-latest electronic gadgets raise our children. Again, I repeat more than 50 percent of marriages end in divorce and 90 percent of all divorced say finances were the biggest contributor to arguments in the marriage. Sadly, the statistics for divorce are the same for Christians as non-Christians. This desperately needs to change!

I personally believe if men would get their financial disciplines in alignment with God's word, get the wives and moms back into the homes, and become godly men treating their wives as outlined by Scriptures, we would see less divorce and more disciplined children that would grow up as respectful and responsible adults. Men, this doesn't mean you must work two or more jobs for most of your life as I did! What is really needed is developing a lifestyle of living within your means. I believe we must change this ungodly cycle, and we must stop greed and fear from controlling our decisions! We must put our faith in God, trust in his provisions, and apply his wisdom in our financial needs. We must learn that:

🗝 God will provide for our needs if we are faithful and will trust in him!

> Therefore I say unto you, Take no thought for your life, what ye shall eat, or what ye shall drink; nor yet for your body, what ye shall put on. Is not the life more than meat, and the body than raiment? Behold the fowls of the air: for they sow not, neither do they reap, nor gather into barns; yet your heavenly Father feedeth them. Are ye not much better than they?
>
> Matthew 6:25–26 (KJV)

It is not God's plan for you to be overly concerned about your needs. God cares about you, and he has already made provisions for your needs. It has been said that worry is the indicator of taking ownership of something that belongs to God. Ownership belongs to God, and he is faithful to provide if we are faithful to apply his word. He cares about you and will make provisions for your needs to be met. Don't get me wrong! God certainly expects us to work and provide for our families if we are able.

The Apostle Paul said:

> But if any provide not for his own, and specially for those of his own house, he hath denied the faith, and is worse than an infidel.
>
> 1 Timothy 5:8 (KJV)

Sadly, there are those who will not work and then believe the church is supposed to feed and clothe them. However, Paul gives strict instructions to the church not to support those that will not work. This is not cruel! Hunger is a good motivation to find work.

> For even when we were with you, this we commanded you, that if any would not work, neither should he eat.
>
> 2 Thessalonians 3:10 (KJV)

However, we must be careful not to establish a lifestyle that requires excessive work to the point of not having quality family time or that is above our means to support. Living within your means is a must. It is God's way! If you are currently living above your means and are burdened with debt, there is hope for your financial situation.

🔑 **God can and will set you free from the bondage of debt if you are willing to change, have a heart of repentance, seek wise, godly counsel, and apply disciplines and accountability.**

Why do so many people get in debt? I have been teaching and counseling on finances since 1986 and find most people are in debt because of one or more of the following reasons:

🔑 Lack of wisdom and discipline

Our culture influences us to get it, and get it now. So we borrow to appease our lack of money and lack of patience. We don't discipline ourselves to live within our means. If we lived like most of our great grandparents that lived during the depression, we probably would see no title loan companies or payday loan companies, no credit cards, and fewer loan companies of any sort.

🔑 Bad decisions and bad habits

Bad decisions and bad habits are manifested in wanting conveniences we cannot afford, personal addictions, and investments we cannot afford. This destructive cycle can be broken.

🔑 Gather facts and pray to make good decisions!

It is important before we make decisions that we get all the facts we can. We must determine what real needs are versus wants. We must evaluate our resources. Most importantly, we need to pray about what we do. Inquiring of God seems to have lost its place in the decision making process. But all through the Bible, we see men inquiring of God prior to making major decisions. We also see examples where men failed to inquire of God, and they made bad decisions that not only cost them greatly but also cost the following generations. For Christians, there is wisdom and safety in bringing everything before God and waiting on God to answer prior to making a final decision.

🔑 Develop good habits and free yourself from addictions to get out of debt.

One of the hardest obstacles to overcome is bad habits! I can't tell you the number of people that can't pay rent or buy groceries or keep the lights on but refuse to give up their conveniences and personal addictions or even investments they can't afford. If you are destitute you must be willing to sacrifice nonessentials. You must be willing to do whatever is necessary to become free of addictions. God will put men or women in your life to help you if your heart is right with him.

🔑 Others cannot help you if you are unwilling to help yourself!

Unless you are willing to change, no advice or financial assistance will fix your financial problem. Unwillingness to change shows a spiritual problem that must be dealt with first to experience a permanent fix to your financial problem.

🔑 **Never invest into what you don't understand, what you can't afford to lose, or that which will put you into bondage to stay financially free!**

When we talk about investments, our thoughts turn to the stock market. But investments are extended unto anything we accumulate. Often, people make bad investments for lack of knowledge and understanding.

Some people like to collect antiques or other collectables, and that is not bad if you can afford it. Some talk about the value of their collections as investments while they are deeply indebted or making great sacrifices. My young son collected baseball cards and one day was telling me how much some cards were worth. I chuckled and told him it didn't matter what the books said they were worth. Their real value is determined when someone deposits a certain amount of money into his hand at the time he sells them. Those investing in the stock market understand it's really not about what the market says today. Tomorrow the price could increase or fall greatly! What really counts is what you actually receive when you sell. I'm not against investments. In fact, I encourage investing for the future, but a wise man once told me that you should never invest into something you know nothing about. He also told me don't invest money you can't afford to lose in risky adventures. I personally invested in mutual funds through a former employer retirement account. Now that I have less than ten years until retirement, I realized I can't afford another market crash. Since I don't have the time or the knowledge to invest wisely in the markets, I secured a godly financial advisor to advise me in investing my retirement funds and then I prayed and heard from God. Although, the advisor's plan was a good plan for most people, God's plan for Ann and me was different. My advice to anyone is to seek godly knowledgeable advisors that can evaluate your entire needs and help direct you to achieve the optimal results. But take whatever they recommend before the Lord in prayer and hear his plan. He may say this is right for you, or he may give you an entirely different way as he did me.

🔑 Major life circumstances

We are all subject to circumstance in our lives that are out of our control. A few people are in debt because of extenuating circumstances such as illness they could not possibly financially prepare for.

In these circumstances, the bible is plain that *first*, our blood family is responsible to assist provided you have already done everything you can. Then second, our church family is to step in and offer assistance that is above and beyond the ability of what the blood family can do. This is another reason you should have a local church where you are faithful to attend and to serve. Along with committing your heart and life to God, attending and involving yourself in a local church ministry is vital to your overall spiritual, mental, and physical being. If you are going through a major life circumstance, you should let your family know and also go to your pastor and share your need. Your pastor can seek discernment from God to determine what God desires the blood family and the family of God to do. As a previous counselor at my local church, I'm amazed at the individuals that never enter the doors of a local church until they are in financial need. But when a financial crisis arises, they look for a church for assistance. They expect the church to support their bad habits and lack of discipline. This is where it requires real discernment and discipline by the minister to address the real need of salvation and godly disciplines.

🔑 Misguided financial help to others

This is common where people have helped families or friends that have been poor stewards and now find themselves in a financial crisis. I have learned during my tenure of counseling that intervening and financially bailing someone out of a situation where God is trying to bring correction to them and draw them to him, God can, and often will, turn his attention to you and remove your resources to help them so he can continue his work upon the person you were trying to bailed out. I have also learned that intervening when God is at work in others' life slows the correction process and makes it even harder for the person you were trying to help. Discernment is desperately needed in giving financial assistance including when it is a family member. We must understand God's complete plan is to redeem that person, and he will do whatever is necessary to give that person opportunity to repent.

Scriptures are plain that we are to help the poor and the needy; but we must understand why they are poor and needy and the condition of their heart. It takes discernment to know whom we are to help and when we are to help. You should always pray for directions about helping someone. When it is discerned that God is working on an individual, you should wait on God's instruction to give financial assistance. When they have truly repented then God may instruct you to come to their financial assistance.

When I was an insurance agent, we were instructed that most widow women were broke within eighteen months after receiving benefits from their husband's life insurance policy because family and friends came with their sad stories. I've known where a woman received a lump-sum of money and the family members shared their sad stories with her. She assisted and soon she was in financial need herself. Widows, there is great safety to get under independent, godly counsel when you lose your spouse and receive death benefits. Likewise, I would advise the same to any single woman receiving a lump-sum of money. God has given many women a tender and merciful heart, Satan will try to use anyone he can to steal what you have so as to destroy your joy in the Lord. These family members may have had good intentions to pay you back, but because of their poor stewardship, you probably will never see that money again. Always pray about everything, and seek wise, godly counsel.

🔑 Loss of Job

There was a time in the history of our nation that you got a job and stayed on that job until you retired. That is no longer true in America today. You should never live in fear of losing your job, but you also should not be so foolish as to never prepare for a possible layoff. There is a good chance you will not work with your present employer until you retire. I worked for the same employer for almost twenty-two years. Then wham! I walked in early one morning to get a head start on some issues I knew were pending, but before I could sit down at my desk, the phone rang. It was my supervisor requesting me to come to his office. When I arrived, he informed me that I was permanently laid off.

It can happen to anyone! Prepare as best as possible for the unexpected. This was the second layoff I experienced and came only ten years after the first layoff! Thankfully, at this time in my life I had financially prepared myself. The extended time before reemployment can be beyond any savings you might have. The person with no savings is in trouble from the start. Currently at the writing of this book, it is taking approximately twelve months or more for a person to find a job paying even close to their previous salary.

Savings are a must have! Many financial advisors are advising having a minimum of twelve months or more of living expenses in savings. Because I believe in trusting God, I personally advise having at least four months of living expenses in a savings account. When I say "living expenses," I mean what is necessary for survival. Having an adequate savings account gives you a period of time to make major adjustments in your lifestyle, and at the same time, doesn't allow for you to get idle in aggressively searching for work. At any rate, don't let unemployment catch you off guard!

🔑 It's a family problem!

By this I use the term of generational bondage.

> And the LORD passed by before him, and proclaimed, The LORD, The LORD God, merciful and gracious, longsuffering, and abundant in goodness and truth, Keeping mercy for thousands, forgiving iniquity and transgression and sin, and that will by no means clear the guilty; visiting the iniquity of the fathers upon the children, and upon the children's children, unto the third and to the fourth generation.
>
> Exodus 34:6–7 (KJV)

In the many years that I have counseled families, there have been many times I can trace the same habits, symptoms, and problems to the parents, grandparents, and even to the great grandparents. This is sadly true even among Christians. One of the first biblical things for us to do is to examine ourselves and ask God to reveal unto us why we are doing what we do or why we are going through what we are going through. There may be things in our past that are affecting our present behaviors.

Notice in this passage, God says he forgives our iniquities, transgression, and sin. But God also says the iniquities will follow up unto the fourth generation. God was speaking to his chosen people in this passage. Christians, the same is true for you. This is a spiritual stronghold in the heart that must be torn down.

Iniquity is simply doing it our way or any other way rather than God's way. A lot of things we innocently do are because it is the way our parents did it. That does not make it God's way. We must measure it against God's word. It is very important we understand what we say and what we do has a powerful influence on our children and our grandchildren. We establish a foundation or pattern for future generations. Generational bondage is *real*! However, you can break the curse today. How?

🔑 **Turn to God, repent, confess your forefathers' and your fault, seek his deliverance, and receive his word. God can change you! He can set you free!**

Ask yourself if your parents and grandparents financial situation was the same as yours? If the answer is yes, then there is a generational bondage in your family. Often, those I counsel immediately recognize the connection. Perhaps, today, you recognize this generational bondage in your family. Do you want to break it and be free from this bondage? It can happen! You must have a heart of repentance and develop disciplines in alignment with God's word to live within your income.

🔑 **Basic needs expense must be within the husband's income!**

This is an area that gets most families in trouble from the beginning of their marriage. If your living standard requires both spouses income, you are setting yourself up for a financial fall. Basic needs must be supported by the husband's income, and then conveniences can be safely bought from the wife's income. If for some reason, the wife is unable to work, you can safely fall back on basic needs without a financial crisis. You may not think this will ever happen. But let's face it, there is a great possibility the wife is going to get pregnant, and that may require her to be out of work for an extended time. If your basic needs and debts require her income, the accumulated bills will only compound. Now you only have one income to live off, and your savings can quickly deplete. Even if she does return to work, unless she is making a lot of money, it is very difficult to recover from her absence in the workforce. Usually by about eighteen months you are in financial trouble. This is a reality!

Where basic needs cost exceed the husband's income, you will need to downsize, especially housing and vehicles. Conveniences can easily be dropped due to the wife's lost income. Televisions, computers, cable TV, and cell phones are all examples of conveniences you can live without. If the wife does work, let her income buy conveniences that can easily be divested and especially make sure you put a large percent of her income into savings.

🔑 God is the owner of everything!

> The earth is the LORD's, and the fulness thereof; the world, and they that dwell therein.
>
> Psalm 24:1 (KJV)

This is the first Scripture I require those I counsel to memorize. It probably is one of the hardest to absorb in our inner being and apply in our actions. If this truth doesn't get embedded into your mind you will always struggle in making the right financial choices. God doesn't leave out anything! David recognized God owns it all. God says he owns your spouse, your children, your house, your car, your money, everything you see, hear, touch, and smell. Everything belongs to him. This is taught as a biblical principle, but it is more than a principle. It is God's law, whether we recognize it or not! We can't change it. Principles are rules of thumb that can change given the circumstances, but regardless of the situation, everything always belongs to God. A thief may come into your house and steal your television. He takes possession of it, but is he the owner? No! Does he have the right to do with it as he pleases? No! Likewise, what we have in our possession belongs to God. When we disregard this fact of ownership and do what we please with what he has entrusted into our care, we place ourselves into the same position as the thief. Read Malachi 3:7–12! I know this sounds harsh, but when we steal from God, there are consequences!

🔑 If God is the owner of everything, and he is, then we are stewards of his possessions.

A steward is one who manages the possessions of another. Your banker is a steward of your money held in the bank. How would you like to go to the bank to get your money and the teller says, "I'm sorry, the bank manager used your money to throw the employees a party!" Would you be upset? Of course you would! The banker failed to administer your funds properly and give you a return on your investment. I believe you might even take some action to punish this wrongful behavior. Why would we think God would be any different? God is a God of love, but he also is a God of wrath and righteous justice! All throughout the Bible we see the emotions of God demonstrated! Your spouse, your children, everything in your possession belongs to God, and he has entrusted you to take care of those things for him as his steward!

🔑 Failure to recognize God's ownership will result in poor management, poor disciplines, and bad habits.

Luke chapter 16:1–13 teaches us some valuable lessons of stewardship!

> And he said also unto his disciples, There was a certain rich man, which had a steward; and the same was accused unto him that he had wasted his goods. And he called him, and said unto him, How is it that I hear this of thee? give an account of thy stewardship; for thou mayest be no longer steward. Then the steward said within himself, What shall I do? for my lord taketh away from me the stewardship: I cannot dig; to beg I am ashamed. I am resolved what to do, that, when I am put out of the stewardship, they may receive me into their houses. So he called every one of his lord's debtors unto him, and said unto the first, How much owest thou unto my lord? And he said, An hundred

measures of oil. And he said unto him, Take thy bill, and sit down quickly, and write fifty. Then said he to another, And how much owest thou? And he said, An hundred measures of wheat. And he said unto him, Take thy bill, and write fourscore. And the lord commended the unjust steward, because he had done wisely: for the children of this world are in their generation wiser than the children of light. And I say unto you, Make to yourselves friends of the mammon of unrighteousness; that, when ye fail, they may receive you into everlasting habitations.

Luke 16:1–9 (KJV)

Skipping down to verse 13:

No servant can serve two masters: for either he will hate the one, and love the other; or else he will hold to the one, and despise the other. Ye cannot serve God and mammon.

Luke 16:13 (KJV)

What can we learn from this passage concerning stewardship?

God is going to call us into account one day! We must be wise and diligent about our Father's business! God has given man common sense! You don't need a revelation from God as to what is prudent! There is only one master—money and only money or God and only God!

We may think we are getting by in our present actions, but, truly, there is coming a day God will call each of us in account either in this life or in eternity. God rewards those that diligently administer his affairs. When we have failed, we must immediately repent and do what is right and reasonable. Yes, seek God for wisdom, but also do the things he has already instilled within you. Many people try to live on the fence, but one small movement and you will fall off. Get on one side or the other.

A double minded man is unstable in all his ways.

James 1:8 (KJV)

God's word teaches that you are committed right now to either serve him or to serve the prince of this world, Satan. You can't casually serve God and seek after the things of this world.

🔑 Don't expect God to bail you out of your situation!

You made the mess of your financial situation, and he will let you go through the pain of recovery! He will give you grace, wisdom, and divine provisions as you spiritually progress.

Now let's read verses 10–12:

> He that is faithful in that which is least is faithful also in much: and he that is unjust in the least is unjust also in much. If therefore ye have not been faithful in the unrighteous mammon, who will commit to your trust the true riches? And if ye have not been faithful in that which is another man's, who shall give you that which is your own?
>
> Luke 16:10–12 (KJV)

Why would God give us more if we have mishandled what he has already entrusted unto us?

I'm stubborn. I spent seventeen days of a twenty-one-day fast asking God to give me more money! Finally, I got it right spiritually. I began asking God to give me wisdom to use what he had already given me. When I showed God I was using wisdom with what I had, he then started blessing me with more, and I sought wisdom in how to use it also.

🔑 More money is not the answer! Right attitude and proper use of what you have is the answer!

I told you earlier that if I could pay off all your debts today, in approximately eighteen to thirty-six months from now, you would be back in the same debt situation. Why? It's because you have not changed your attitude and actions to be in alignment with God's word and plan for your life. You will continue to do the same things and make the same mistakes until there is a transformation of you mind. From the fall of man, our minds have been corrupted. God's thoughts and ways are 180 degrees from man's ways.

> For my thoughts are not your thoughts, neither are your ways my ways, saith the Lord. For as the heavens are higher than the earth, so are my ways higher than your ways, and my thoughts than your thoughts.
>
> Isaiah 55:8–9 (kjv)

🔑 **We must learn God's ways. Our minds must be renewed if we are to change our ways!**

> And be not conformed to this world: but be ye transformed by the renewing of your mind, that ye may prove what is that good, and acceptable, and perfect, will of God.
>
> Romans 12:2 (kjv)

In this chapter, I have only briefly touched on some of the lessons Ann and I have learned. There is so much more God desires to teach you. I have addressed some valuable key lessons you need to learn to change your attitude and prepare for action changes. In the next chapters, I'm going to give you some simple biblical and practical keys Ann and I applied that got us out of debt. Again, I have shared these with others, and those that have followed them have experienced the same results of coming out from under debt bondage as Ann and me!

Pray this prayer before proceeding to the next chapter,

> God, in the name of Jesus, I come before you. I thank you for what I have experienced! I thank you for the provisions you have given! I confess that I have not been a good steward of your possessions! I have erred from your word in handling money! I have put myself and my family in

bondage. Change my heart, Oh God! Give me a listening heart! Give me the wisdom from this moment forward to manage your possessions. I commit to listen and obey your written word, your Holy Spirit, and the wise counsel of godly men. In the name of Jesus. Amen.

SPIRITUAL KEYS FOR GETTING OUT OF DEBT

In previous chapters, I gave you some important spiritual keys to lay a foundation for spiritual change. Most debt crises are the symptoms of a greater spiritual problem. Therefore, a change of heart and application of God's word is necessary for a permanent solution to get out of debt and stay out of debt. In this chapter, I will address additional spiritual keys we learned and put in place to get out of debt and stay out of debt!

These keys are very simple to understand but essential to develop a lifestyle of change. Hopefully, these spiritual keys will energize your mind and spirit, motivate you to meditate upon them, come to a conviction, and act with a mindset for change and commitment to put them into application.

🔑 There must be a moment of truth!

By this, I mean you must admit your personal contribution to your financial crisis. It didn't just happen. Your accumulated long and short term decisions and your actions contributed to the financial crisis. You must be truthful to yourself as to how you got into debt. People with addictions cannot get deliverance until they truly recognize and confess they are addicted to substances or even bad habits and develop disciplines to protect themselves from their addictions! Likewise, you must recognize your role in your debt crisis, and you must identify how your decisions and habits have contributed and then develop disciplines to protect yourself. God's word teaches a principle that can also be applied for buying on credit!

> Abstain from all appearance of evil.
>
> 1 Thessalonians 5:22 (KJV)

If you don't want to be tempted to get further in debt by buying a car on credit, simply stay off car lots and don't look at ads for cars. Just because it's a holiday and all the stores are offering sales, it doesn't mean you have to go window shopping. If you have a weakness for sales using your credit card, only go to the store when you need something and have cash in hand. If you must go window shopping, leave you credit cards at home.

🔑 Recognize the spiritual problem!

How we manage money is an indicator of what is going on in our heart. There could be several spiritual problems in your heart that effect your debt situation. Living within your means is biblical! When you don't, there is a spiritual problem.

An over abundance of things is a symptom of the spiritual problem of greed! Many of us will not admit we have a problem with greed, but in truth, this is a real problem in America. Advertisers understand this and flood the airwaves and print with ads enticing you to satisfy your hearts desires. Greed manifests itself through the addiction of excessive spending. We live in a generation where we must have it, and we must have it now! It must be the biggest and the best! It is buy now and pay later, and, boy, do you pay! It is not uncommon for many people to have three to five credit cards charged to their limit. Most major stores offer some kind of in house credit card. They know if you have their card, they have a tool to easily convince you to buy now and they can up sell to the bigger and costlier items and then add on accessories and extended warranties. I personally believe it is better to assume the risk and stick with the manufacturer's warranty rather than buying extended warranties. You can insure yourself to the poor house. Excessive spending and over protection is an abandonment of trusting in God's provisions and protection.

Rent to own stores are everywhere and are very profitable businesses. These businesses target the poor and the undisciplined to fill their needs and desires. Yes, they offer payment plans to make it easier to immediately obtain items you want or need, but in the end you could pay twice the price or more for an item. These businesses and their payment plans entice you to purchase more expensive items and greater quantities than you should and can really afford. Is this good stewardship? I think not!

Additionally, payday quick loan companies and title loan companies can give you that quick cash—but at what cost? Repossessions, extending payments with exorbitant interest rates and penalties, bad credit reporting, not to mention, just paying too much for that quick cash fix are some of the problems encountered by those using these companies. After talking to the clerk at one title loan company, I realized they were charging 131 percent interest plus the late penalties. This in my opinion is highway robbery and taking advantage of the poor! I told the clerk I didn't know how they could live with themselves in charging such fees. I later learned this amount of interest and even more was common among these type loan companies. No wonder the South Carolina state representatives where I live were trying to shut down these companies. However, these companies have a lot of money, and so it didn't happen. If you are going to these type businesses, you really have a problem. They are not the solution. You are treating the symptoms rather than fixing the problem. God has the solution for you!

Greed also manifests itself through the addiction of hoarding.

Open you closet, your attic, your garage, your storage building. It could be hazardous to your health! It is amazing how much people accumulate. Have you ever watched those house cleaning programs where there was a trail to the bed and bathroom? You can't see the kitchen counters or the floor and then there was just enough room to sit or lay down in a small space on the bed. Many times, much of the items had to be thrown away because of bacteria, mold, mice infestation, or just plain rot. Is this good stewardship? I think not!

This is not just a physical problem; this is a real spiritual problem!

We are convinced we need things we seldom or never use and so we store them. Some people are so addicted to buying things and storing them that it requires spiritual counseling to get free from this bondage of hoarding. Many years ago, I developed a two-year rule of thumb. I try to practice and advise others to do the same. If it is not used within two years, sell it! Place the money in a jar or bank savings account and hold it there until you need to use the item and then go rent it or buy another. If you buy it, you can turn around and sell it! The normal exception for this rule would be if the item is a family heirloom. But in extreme financial crises, it may be necessary to sell even these items. Don't worry, your family will not roll over in their graves! If they were alive they would tell you that you are more important than things and to get out of debt no matter what you might have to sacrifice!

🗝 Confess that you do not have the wisdom to straighten out your financial affairs.

How long have you been trying to get out of debt only to find you seem to be getting further in debt? I tried for five years to get out of debt. Men are stubborn and resist admitting they can't fix the problem. As a benevolence minister at my local church, I found that 99 percent of the time it was the wife that came in first to seek financial assistance. Sometimes, the husband would be sitting in the car. I would just go to the car and meet him and invite him to come in before I would consider financial assistance. I knew that, more than likely, he was the main contributor to the financial crisis. Women buy a lot of small things, but men buy big ticket items like houses, cars, motorcycles, boats, and other recreational vehicles and equipment. Yes, in my opinion most women have too many shoes in their closet, but in reality it is the big ticket items that will ultimately bring you to a financial crisis. I will say that excess, whether it is too many shoes or big ticket items that you can't afford, is the symptom of a spiritual problem!

🗝 You must seek and ask God to give you wisdom.

> If any of you lack wisdom, let him ask of God, that giveth to all men liberally, and upbraideth not; and it shall be given him.
>
> James 1:5 (KJV)

I repeat this key again because it is so important in the process of getting out of debt. Being in debt is a symptom of making wrong choices. You can't rely on what you think is best! Before you act, ask God what he would have you to do.

🗝 Don't just ask, hear what God has to say!

We may pray a lot of prayers, and they may be long prayers, but, sometimes, we need to be as the publican in Luke 18:13 and beat our chest and say "God have mercy on me!" and then shut up and wait on God to speak to us. He still speaks to men! Often we just fail to hear him speaking because we are not listening. Have you ever been in a situation where you were talking to someone and maybe your child said something to you? You didn't give them your undivided attention, and so you may have responded but never really heard what they were saying. It is important when we pray at some moment we stop praying, and then give God our undivided attention and let him speak to us.

🗝 Let the Holy Spirit speak.

God likes to communicate with his children. For some reason, God likes to wake me between 1 a.m. and 3 a.m. Maybe it's because this is the only time he can get my full attention! If you are not hearing God speak, this is a spiritual problem because God still speaks to men in our generation.

How does the Holy Spirit speak to us?

He speaks through the written word.

The most complete book of wisdom is God's written word. Although every situation is not specifically mentioned in the Bible, there are principles that will apply to every area of our lives. If you don't read the Bible regularly, God will not speak wisdom to you from his word. I have heard Christians make the statement "the Bible is too hard to understand!"

I get excited as I read the following passage to know God desires to bless his people beyond our imagination and he desires to reveal the hidden treasures of his word.

> But as it is written, Eye hath not seen, nor ear heard, neither have entered into the heart of man, the things which God hath prepared for them that love him. But God hath revealed them unto us by his Spirit: for the Spirit searcheth all things, yea, the deep things of God. For what man knoweth the things of a man, save the spirit of man which is in him? even so the things of God knoweth no man, but the Spirit of God. Now we have received, not the spirit of the world, but the spirit which is of God; that we might know the things that are freely given to us of God. Which things also we speak, not in the words which man's wisdom teacheth, but which the Holy Ghost teacheth; comparing spiritual things with spiritual. But the natural man receiveth not the things of the Spirit of God: for they are foolishness unto him: neither can he know them, because they are spiritually discerned. But he that is spiritual judgeth all things, yet he himself is judged of no man. For who hath known the

mind of the Lord, that he may instruct him? But we have the mind of Christ.

1 Corinthians 2:9–16 (KJV)

We are constantly reminded the bible is a spiritual book. Understanding only comes from developing a deep relationship with God and it is given according to God's timing and through the Holy Spirit. We learned as a child that we can only put so much food in our mouths and be able to chew it and swallow. Likewise, God knows just how much understanding to give to us at various points in our walk with him.

He speaks audibly.

I have heard others talk about hearing God speak to them. On a few occasions, God has spoken audibly to me; not a conversation but simple words or sentences. I remember one night, God woke me from my sleep and said, "Remember, remember, remember." I knew exactly what he was telling me. Our church was going through some changes, and we were praying for directions. God was reminding me of things he had already given us to do, and he was reminding us to do what he had already instructed us to do.

The audible voice of God is not something new. Why should we think it so strange when someone says God spoke to them? God has spoken audibly to man beginning in the garden and throughout the Old Testament and even the New Testament.

> And after the earthquake a fire; but the LORD was not in the fire: and after the fire a still small voice. And it was so, when Elijah heard it, that he wrapped his face in his mantle, and went out, and stood in the entering in of the cave. And, behold, there came a voice unto him, and said, What doest thou here, Elijah?
>
> 1 Kings 19:12–13(KJV)

And,

> As they ministered to the Lord, and fasted, the Holy Ghost said, Separate me Barnabas and Saul for the work whereunto I have called them.
>
> Acts 13:2 (KJV)

God has not stopped speaking to man! He will speak to you! When you hear the voice of God speaking, it changes your life. You yearn to hear him more. You receive an extra measure of faith! No one can take God's word from you. Be humble. You are not something extra special compared to other Christians, just one of his children who has developed an ear to hear. God desires to speak to you. Will you listen?

He speaks through dreams and visions.

The Bible is full of examples where God spoke to his servants through dreams and gave the prophets visions of the future. Again, God seemingly likes to deal with me in the early morning hours. Most of the time, the dreams and visions are very pleasant and very exciting. Sometimes, they are very disturbing as they are warnings for a particular situation or person. Sometimes, God put conditions upon a vision for it to be fulfilled. My problem is when God gives me a word or vision, I desire to see the fulfillment immediately, but it often happens sometime in the distant future. Just look at the visions of the prophets of Old. Some took many years and some are still waiting fulfillment. Don't despair when God shows you something and you don't see it coming to pass as God has a timing for all things. A wise minister taught me that a seed has to die before it lives and so do visions. Remember, if God spoke it, then it will happen! Sometimes, God gives me warnings or a word for the body of Christ or for my family. He can and will do the same for you if you prepare to receive his word.

He speaks directly to our minds and our spirit.

Recently, I was praying about a situation, and all of a sudden, this thought just came to my mind. It was like, "Have you considered this?" This has happened on many occasions. Most likely, it has happened to you too. When my teenage son moved out on his own, there was an incident where he was hijacked. My wife and I were about to go to bed, when all of a sudden, God spoke into my spirit that we urgently needed to pray for Chris. We both knelt beside the couch and begin pouring out our hearts. We did not know why we were praying but only that Chris needed our earnest prayers. I don't know just how long we prayed, but it was for some time. We finally got peace in our spirit and went to bed. The next morning, we learned about him being hijacked. For some reason, the hijacker had Chris drive to a house and told him to wait while the hijacker went inside. The hijacker told Chris he would be watching and would kill him if he moved. My son said that as soon as the hijacker went through the door, he threw the car in reverse and jumped a ditch to get away. Chris told us the time he got away, and it was the same time we finally got peace in our spirit! I believe in intercessory prayer and believe to this day our Chris is alive because we listened to the voice of God and interceded for Chris. We had similar experiences concerning our daughter Angela.

Satan is out to kill, steal, and destroy your family. God cares about you and your family and will speak into your spirit when Satan is on the prowl. Develop a listening ear and heart for God's voice.

> My sheep hear my voice, and I know them, and they follow me:
>
> John 10:27 (KJV)

Let me clarify a point when I talk about God speaking to us: We have all heard the outrageous stories where someone declared that God told them to do some evil act. This is pure nonsense! God never contradicts his word. However, Satan and his angels will imitate the things of God and will try to deceive you into believing God spoke something contradictory to his character and his word. Let me make it clear, God will never contradict his character and his word!

When Jesus was here on earth, he declared:

> Then said Jesus unto them, When ye have lifted up the Son of man, then shall ye know that I am he, and that I do nothing of myself; but as my Father hath taught me, I speak these things.
>
> John 8:28 (KJV)

Jesus never instructed his followers outside of God's divine word. Likewise, the Holy Spirit only speaks according to God's word.

> But the Comforter, which is the Holy Ghost, whom the Father will send in my name, he shall teach you all things, and bring all things to your remembrance, whatsoever I have said unto you.
>
> John 14:26 (KJV)

Did you really hear from God? If what is given agrees with God's written word, it came from God. If it disagrees with God's written word, it came from a lying spirit. There are a lot of lying spirits in the world today. Some are cloaked in a minister's or teacher's garments. What they say makes sense, it sounds good, but it is damnable.

> For such are false apostles, deceitful workers, transforming themselves into the apostles of Christ. And no marvel; for Satan himself is transformed into an angel of light. Therefore it is no great thing if his ministers also be transformed as the ministers of righteousness; whose end shall be according to their works.
>
> 2 Corinthians 11:13–15 (KJV)

False prophets and teachers where everywhere, even during the life of Paul, and he knew after his death it would get worst. He again instructed the Roman Christians.

> Now I beseech you, brethren, mark them which cause divisions and offences contrary to the doctrine which ye have learned; and avoid them. [18] For they that are such serve not our Lord Jesus Christ, but their own belly; and by good words and fair speeches deceive the hearts of the simple.
>
> Romans 16:17 (KJV)

God knew the devices Satan would use to deceive us, and thus, he breathed his infallible truth into the spirit of holy men. He gave us his word as a standard of truth to expose deceit, to align us to his ways and his thoughts, and to instruct us in our daily walk toward our promise land with the reward of life eternal.

> All scripture is given by inspiration of God, and is profitable for doctrine, for reproof, for correction, for instruction in righteousness:
>
> 2 Timothy 3:16 (KJV)

Unless you are a student of God's written word and have an intimate relationship with God, you can and will be deceived.

He speaks through the words of others.

Especially through his anointed ministers! Have you ever been sitting in church or Bible class and all of a sudden, understanding of a passage came as a minister spoke? It should be that when a minister enters the pulpit, he has a word from God to the congregation. Sadly, I've heard of ministers who never pick up the Bible or quote a Scripture. Some have even used publications like *Readers Digest* or other magazines to formulate a message. I don't know about you, but I desire to know in my spirit that the minister has been before God and has a message from God to draw my heart closer to God and to change my ways for the good.

Moses, Nathan, Elijah even Jonah are examples of men of the Old Testament who received specific messages to be delivered to others. Peter and Paul and the other writers delivered messages in the New Testament days. These messages are etched in eternity as they are direct words from God.

🔑 Commit to obey and apply God's wisdom!

> But be ye doers of the word, and not hearers only, deceiving your own selves. For if any be a hearer of the word, and not a doer, he is like unto a man beholding his natural face in a glass: For he beholdeth himself, and goeth his way, and straightway forgetteth what manner of man he was. But whoso looketh into the perfect law of liberty, and continueth therein, he being not a forgetful hearer, but a doer of the work, this man shall be blessed in his deed.
>
> James 1:22–25

It's one thing to hear wisdom and it's another to apply it in our lives. Failing to apply that which is spoken shows a lack of commitment and trust in God. God cares for us and as a parent desires the best for us. We may not always understand at that moment, but if we will trust him and apply his word, we will see victory.

🔑 Seek wise spiritual counsel!

> Without counsel purposes are disappointed: but in the multitude of counsellors they are established.
>
> Proverbs 15:22 (KJV)

The word of God has a lot to say about counsel. I believe it is because man, if left to himself, will fail every time.

> There is a way that seemeth right unto a man, but the end thereof are the ways of death.
>
> Proverbs 16:25 (KJV)

God has provided many individuals in your life to give you godly counsel.

Your spouse is the most important counselor God has placed in your life especially if they are godly. Still, don't count them out even if they are not a Christian. If God spoke through a donkey, he can even speak wisdom to you through the *non-Christian* spouse. Men like to be the decision makers, but hear me, men! God uses your spouse to give you spiritual wisdom in a decision making process. God intended for her to be your helpmate, and that includes helping to come to a conclusion of what must be done or not done. Often, if the wife is reluctant to accept an idea or deal, it can be because God is giving them a warning that it is a bad idea or deal. When the spouse is reluctant, you must open your mind and listen to see if God is speaking through your spouse.

God will also speak wisdom through your minister, your Christian financial advisor or budget counselor, friends and family, and even strangers.

Don't limit God to what is comfortable! I have found God works through people we would reject, and he works in mysterious ways.

🔑 Set up a system of accountability with a third party!

> Confess your faults one to another, and pray one for another, that ye may be healed. The effectual fervent prayer of a righteous man availeth much.
>
> James 5:16 (KJV)

Accountability deals with your pride, it humbles you and gives you a prayer partner. We don't like showing our dirty laundry to others. Men, especially, will make verbal commitments that they will do what is right up front. However, in all the years of my counseling, when the going gets tough, rarely have I seen men who will follow through without being accountable to a third party.

It is important that the third party should not be your spouse. Why? Because I have found one spouse usually dominates the other. Sometimes, it is the husband; and sometimes, it is the wife. In this situation, the dominated spouse can't hold you accountable. Find a friend or minister that cares about you and will tell you the truth, usually, what you don't want to hear when you are about to make a bad decision. Don't get me wrong, your spouse should be party to ever significant decision as that decision will also affect them. God made you one and you should function as one.

🔑 Report on a regular schedule to the accountability party.

Husbands and wives should sit together weekly at first to examine their expenditures and spending. Together, they should identify success areas and problem areas and develop a strategy to correct any problems. Prayer is essential during this process to find unity and solutions. Instead of finances being the main contributor to arguments, this time should be one of developing oneness and respect for one other. This can also be a teachable time for children. Get them involved. It will cause you less grief down the road in their wants and desires and will teach them at an early age about managing money God's way. Spouses together should then meet with the third party advisor at least biweekly during the first three months and progress to monthly, quarterly, and then annual meetings or as needed to get further discernment and correction or confirmation.

🔑 Set up parameters.

The accountability party must have liberty to rebuke and set up penalties, and you must agree to abide by their decision. Otherwise, you are wasting their time, and you will continue doing the wrong things just adding to the crisis. If you find yourself getting angry with your accountability party, it is probably because your flesh desires to override godly instructions. Ask yourself if this person really care about you. What have they really got to gain out of troubling your spirit by telling you something you don't desire to hear? This is a Holy Spirit moment of conviction!

🗝 Set up penalties for noncompliance.

Children should learn early that noncompliance to parental instructions will cost them dearly. Just because you are an adult, doesn't mean there should not be penalties for failure to comply with sound godly wisdom and God's infallible word. God gives us permission to go ahead and do what we desire. But he also informs us of the penalty of sin.

> Behold, all souls are mine; as the soul of the father, so also the soul of the son is mine: the soul that sinneth, it shall die.
>
> Ezekiel 18:4 (KJV)

The penalty for not complying with a financial plan or our personal, spiritual, and physical disciplines must cost you something that you don't want to give up for it to be effective. God doesn't want *part* of us to serve him—he wants *all* of us or nothing. This is a commitment. Likewise, we must commit to sacrifice things of great value to us to break bad habits and develop good disciplines. When it starts really costing you personally, you will find those bad habits will quickly disappear. If bad habits don't disappear, your sacrifice is a token rather than a real sacrifice. You must *sacrifice* to the hurt! It must be something that cost you and not your family. After all, if you break the rules, it has already cost your family. It must be personal and something you really don't want to do. Maybe, you give up your budgeted weekly allowance for a specific time, or you do chores your spouse would normally do. You might sell something of yours to recoup cost of noncompliance! You could volunteer personal time for an activity of a charitable organization every time you don't comply. You could mow the neighbor's yard or something similar. If it is something you don't want to do, and you will commit to doing it every time you fail. I guarantee, it will not take long to kick the habit. You're not a fool. You will stop the suffering and the hurt by changing the bad behavior.

🔑 Change of attitude and heart are essential.

> And be not conformed to this world: but be ye transformed by the renewing of your mind, that ye may prove what is that good, and acceptable, and perfect, will of God.
>
> Romans 12:2 (KJV)

This key is *essential* for success. It is one of the hardest to obtain without feeding your mind and spirit with the word of God and having a daily relationship and commitment with God.

🔑 Stinking thinking produces stinking results.

You will continue to do the same things until your heart is in alignment with God's word and you are submissive to the Holy Spirit of God. If what you have been doing is not working and has given you bad results, then why would you continue thinking and doing the same things? It's time to change the way you think.

Our attitude must change and will only change when we do the following:

- Seek a deeper relationship with God.
- When we study his word.
- When we ask for wisdom.
- When we commit to hear and obey the Holy Spirit of God.
- When we set means of accountability.

🔑 Bankruptcy is not the option!

Many seem to think this is the easiest method of getting out of debt. However, bankruptcy has its negatives. The government has made it much harder to file for bankruptcy. You can only file once every seven years. The problem is many people are in the same financial situation before the seven years are up. I have personally counseled with individuals that were head over heels in debt within three years of filing bankruptcy. So filing bankruptcy is not the answer! God has given the answer. "Changing your ways and living within your means" is the answer. Another problem with bankruptcy is that it stays on your credit records for at least seven years. However, when you fill out many legal documents, they ask the question, "Have you ever filed bankruptcy?" You really never get away from declaring bankruptcy. I have talked with people that have filed bankruptcy, and their advice was to always avoid bankruptcy like a plague. Laying aside all these reasons, there is one reason that is most important for not filing bankruptcy:

> The wicked borroweth, and payeth not again: but the righteous sheweth mercy, and giveth.
>
> Psalm 37:21 (KJV)

Should Christians be counted with the wicked? No! Let me say there are some situations where creditors will not work with a person, and the only relief to work out a plan is bankruptcy. However, let me warn you in these extreme situations the attitude must be that "I owe this debt and, somehow, by God's grace I'm going to pay it." Then develop a plan that will include sacrifice until it is paid if possible. To do anything less is stealing, and God will not bless a thief.

> But let none of you suffer as a murderer, or as a thief, or as an evildoer, or as a busybody in other men's matters.
>
> 1 Peter 4:15 (KJV)

🔑 Loan consolidation is not the answer!

Again, this is one of the first resources people often turn to when their bills exceed their income. However, because bad habits and attitudes have not changed, loan consolidations usually do not work. What it does do is it gives you enough breathing room and frees up a few dollars so you fall right back into the pattern of making bad decisions. Let's say your TV goes on the blink, and you have a few extra dollars each month. You then go out and buy that fifty-four-inch wide screen TV on credit you have been wanting or something similar. You will justify the purchase and proclaim it was a wise buy that you needed and that deals like this don't happen every day. Before you know it, you don't have enough income again to meet your obligations. Your behavior and attitude have not changed, and you fall back in the same pit of debt bondage. I would beware of many loan consolidation companies as there are reports where they tell you they have worked it out with your creditors only to find later that they failed to make payments leaving you holding the bag and the loss of the commissions you paid to them to manage your money for you. Rather, I suggest you develop an income and expense spreadsheet and contact your creditors to work out a plan of payment yourself or obtain the assistance of a Christian benevolence counselor.

I have given you some spiritual keys for getting out of debt! I'm sure there are many others I have missed, but these alone will lay the foundation you need for mental, spiritual, and physical changes in the way you manage God's possessions. God will give you more directions for your personal situation if you seek his wisdom. In our next chapter, we will submit practical keys for getting out of debt!

In closing this chapter, I would like for you to pray the following prayer. You may have to pray it more than once for it to take hold of your spirit.

Father, I admit I have not been the best steward. I have not been wise, and I have made bad decisions that have caused me and my family grief. I ask for your forgiveness! I will seek your wisdom for future decisions. Holy Spirit, teach me truth! I promise to hear and obey. Father, I will submit to spiritual authority and make myself accountable to you and my brother in Christ. As the Psalmists, prayed I also pray:

Search me, O God, and know my heart: try me, and know my thoughts: And see if there be any wicked way in me, and lead me in the way everlasting.

Psalm 139:23–24

In the name of Jesus, I pray. Amen.

PRACTICAL KEYS FOR GETTING OUT OF DEBT

You may be thinking I should have written only this chapter. However, most people, given the practical keys in this chapter without first empowering the spiritual keys, would most likely return to a financial crisis within eighteen to thirty-six months.

You would be trying to fix a symptom rather than the problem by only implementing the practical keys given in this chapter, and they will not give you a lifetime of living debt-free! There must be a spiritual transformation to remain debt-free. God desires to heal and transform our minds for a better and greater walk in this life. Why should Christians live debt-free? Non-Christians are watching your life. When our walk is similar to the non-Christian, our testimony of God's grace and blessings is distorted. We are to be light not darkness. As Christians, our actions must always point people to the God of our salvation.

> Let your light so shine before men, that they may see your good works, and glorify your Father which is in heaven.
>
> Matthew 5:16 (KJV)

If you skipped any previous chapters, go back now and read them for life changing benefits. It is all part of the process of getting out of debt and staying out of debt.

In this chapter, I will give a brief overview of various programs and methods the world offers for attaining possessions, personal protection, and accumulating wealth. Many of these programs and methods used without spiritual disciplines can put you in spiritual and financial bondage. I'm not an expert in every area I introduce in this chapter; therefore, I advise you to seek wise, godly counsel before making major decisions that will affect your family.

You may not agree with the practical keys or opinions I present. That's okay. My wife, Ann, raised her eyebrows a few times during our journey, but she was submissive, and God blessed us to become and remain debt-free by applying them. You also don't have to understand the reasoning of what I present. However, it's important to put all the applicable keys presented into application. You will understand how necessary each key is to becoming debt-free as you see bills rapidly disappearing.

I believe God answered my prayers and gave me these keys. Ann and I applied the spiritual keys as well as these practical keys and we became and remain debt-free! Your testimony to your family and friends can also be, "I'm debt-free!" They will want to know how you became debt-free, and then my desire will be fulfilled through you as you share the keys with them.

Individuals I have counseled who have applied these same keys have experienced similar results and have had miraculous interventions to occur during their process of getting out of debt just as Ann and I experienced during our journey. Some experienced debt forgiveness and some received additional income and gifts they were not expecting during the process of becoming debt-free. I believe God will do the same or similarly for you if you are faithful to apply all spiritual and practical keys that are applicable to your debt situation.

Remember, what I present is not meant for a one-time crisis; it is a lifestyle change. The goal is debt-free living for life! You can only remain debt-free by thorough, continual application of the spiritual and practical keys presented in this book.

> 🔑 **The spiritual and practical keys used to get out of debt apply for staying out of debt!**

Are you spiritually ready to walk the road of debt-free living? If you have committed to applying the spiritual keys, it's time to learn and apply the practical keys to get that debt monkey off your back.

🔑 Lock the door!

If someone was headed toward your door intending you harm, most likely, you would rush to the door, close it and lock it to protect yourself and your family. Warning: There is an enemy that is out to destroy your very life! It may be your marriage, your children, your health, or whatever you hold close. Regardless of your life's situation, Satan intends to cause you harm and destroy you. He uses the tools that are common to man to create havoc in your life. Debt is one tool Satan uses that is so destructive to your spiritual, emotional, and physical welfare. Now is the time to immediately lock Satan and his devices out of your life!

Locking the door means you:

🔑 Commit not to get further in debt!

You can't get out of debt as long as you continue charging! You must put a stop to charging now! You are in debt! You have lost control! I like what Barney Fife said, "Nip it in the bud!"

You also can't get out of debt without changing what, how, and when to purchase. Too many purchases and you'll find you will be tempted to charge when that big bargain arises. Remember, there must be a lifestyle change!

You lock the door to credit by doing the following:

🔑 Say no to using credit cards for purchases.

Credit cards are not the problem. It is the misuse of credit cards that causes the problem. It was difficult for me to get my first, three-hundred-dollar-limit credit card from my local bank.

However, I was faithful to make the monthly payments on time; therefore, my credit rating increased. Soon my mailbox was bombarded with credit card offers, and I bit the bait offered—hook, line, and sinker. I accumulated credit cards and maxed out each one! I was getting by until, suddenly, my income decreased, and I found myself searching for money to make only the minimum payments. My financial situation was so bad I picked up cans and bottles to sell just to be able to buy gas for my car so I could go to work!

🔑 Make it difficult to use credit cards for purchases.

Developing the discipline not to use credit cards for purchases is very hard for many people. That is especially true if the credit cards are in your wallet! Often, I have advised people to put their credit cards in a secure location such as a locked vehicle dash or the trunk of their car before entering a store. Doing this will hinder impulse buying! When that great bargain is presented, you will have to walk to the car to get your card giving you time to consider what you are doing and to decide if the purchase is worth the future aggravation of being in debt. If you are a hard core credit card user, I would suggest putting your credit cards in a fireproof safe box at home, and keep them there. For many, just having the cards available may be a problem. The best solution is to simply cut all the credit cards into pieces so they can't be used. You can't get further in credit card debt if you don't have them to use. I knew my weakness, and I destroyed my cards at the very beginning. Not having credit cards required me to give more thought to whether the item was a need or want. No credit cards required realistic thought to determine if I had the cash to purchase the item now, or if I had to wait to purchase when I did obtain the money. Not having credit cards was a real blessing for Ann and me; it was the beginning of developing purchasing disciplines. Realistically, I never went back and purchased most of the items when I did have the cash, and I never missed not having those items I would have purchased with a credit card either.

After I developed good, disciplined, spending habits, new credit cards arrived at their renewal time in the mail. However, I called the credit card companies and canceled all but one of the new cards. During this time period, canceling credit cards actually increased your credit score. That is not true today! Canceling credit cards today will decrease your credit score! Put the cards in a safe place, and keep them there or cut them up. Don't send them back to the company as they may cancel your account decreasing your credit score.

Later in this chapter, I will give you practical keys on how to pay off your current credit card balances and the disciplined use of them. Here, I'm emphasizing not to use credit cards at all while you are in debt. Once you are out of debt and only after you have developed good disciplines should you consider using a credit card.

🔑 Warning: The first month you can't pay off the entire balance of a credit card, cut it up!

I remind you again that credit cards are not the problem. The misuse of credit cards is the problem. Proper use of credit cards is treating them like writing a check or using a debit card. You only spend according to budget or your bank balance, not according to the amount of credit you have.

Now that I have developed good disciplines, I buy almost everything on my one credit card and earn airline miles, but I pay the full balance owed each month. My credit card gave Ann and me free round trip air tickets to Arizona for our fortieth anniversary. When I say free, I mean free as we paid no interest on the card because we paid the full balance each month, yet using the card allowed us to earn airline points and so the airline tickets were really free. There are many credit cards that give air miles, merchandise, gift cards, or pay cash back that can be great deals if you never pay the credit card company interest. Again, I warn you that the first month you can't pay off the balance, cut up the card.

Don't apply for new credit card accounts either as this will also decrease your credit score. You may be wondering why, if I'm not going to borrow more money, should I be concerned about my credit score? Insurance companies may use your credit score to determine you insurability and premiums of products they may offer to you. Other companies may offer discounted goods and services depending on your credit score. Some employers use your credit score in determining eligibility for employment with their company. Even though you may have determined to live debt-free, it is still important to maintain good credit scores.

🔑 Say no to ninety days and twelve, eighteen, twenty-four months same as cash plans.

I also fell into these debt traps like many others. With these plans, you have no negotiating power. Retail executives are not fools! Retailers get the price they desire for their merchandise and as an added bonus, they know many people will default on the payment terms; thus, they collect a higher interest rate and interest calculated on full amount of the loan at the beginning date of the contract. It's easy to be late even one day or not make that final payment by the contract date and incur hundreds of dollars in interest. Many times in these same as cash loans, the default finance charges will be 24 percent or higher.

Why avoid same as cash loans? It's because cash money talks! You have much better negotiating power with cash money. You will get the best deal with cash so avoid these same as cash loans.

🔑 Say no to other loans of any type.

Ann and I decided we were not going to buy anything on any type credit while we were digging our way out of our mess. You will never get out of debt if you continue to charge and borrow, and you will never stay out of debt as long as you charge and borrow. Something is going to break or wear out. Later in this and the following chapters, we will give you the keys for proper planning that will assist in preparing for these circumstances.

Now that you have locked the door, it's time to:

🔑 Get the big picture!

God calls us to be accountable in every aspect of our lives, our mind and our actions. We are to be good stewards in planning and maintaining in the present as well as for the future.

> For which of you, intending to build a tower, sitteth not down first, and counteth the cost, whether he have sufficient to finish it? Lest haply, after he hath laid the foundation, and is not able to finish it, all that behold it begin to mock him, Saying, This man began to build, and was not able to finish.
>
> Luke 14:28–30(KJV)

Improper planning usually results in financial crises. To get started on your debt-free journey, you must know your present financial state and lay out a detailed plan to get to where you desire to be. Seeing the big picture involves your present crisis but also gives you the information needed to plan for the future. Getting the big picture requires us to:

🔑 Develop detailed life financial plans.

It is imperative you have a detailed understanding of your assets, income, and expenditures. Only after compiling this information will you be able to develop a plan of action to get out of debt and stay out of debt. This must be done on paper in an organized manner! We have provided in the addendum sample forms you can use to develop your own spread sheets. When done correctly, the life financial plan data becomes a wow experience, and often you can immediately see problem areas as well as some quick fixes to your debt problem. The life financial plan is simply a spread sheet that shows your total monthly income compared to your total monthly expenses. You must take time (with your spouse if you are married) to accumulate all the documentation needed to accurately develop a life financial plan (also known as a budget). Some people don't like the term budget as it seem harsh and restrictive. But a life financial plan is designed to give you the big picture of your financial situation, identify problem areas and develop disciplines and strategies for living within your means and fulfilling God's purpose for wealth.

In order to develop a life financial plan you will need to document in detail.

List your debts. Include creditors' names, monthly payment amounts, balances owed, due dates, and past due amounts. Don't forget to include debts owed to family and friends on this list.

List your income. Include salaries, retirement, interest, dividends, gifts, as well as any other types of income.

List all your assets. Include checking account balances, savings account balances, CDs, cash on hand, investments, 401, 403, IRAs, Roth IRAs, mutual funds, stocks, bonds, properties (houses, land, buildings, jewelry, art, any collectables, anything of significant value), transportation vehicles (cars, trucks, motorcycles), recreational vehicles (ATVs, campers), aircrafts, or any other thing of monetary value.

Track current spending habits. Most often, the first discipline I implement to those I counsel is to require the individuals to track every expense of twenty-five cents or more for the first thirty days. This alone identifies waste and helps the individual to develop a mind-set of discipline. It also gives more accurate detailed information to document on the life financial plan. Couples find their estimates of what they spend on miscellaneous items are far less than their actual expenses.

You will need all the above information to make informed decisions and to develop a life financial plan. Often, you can't see the big picture because you are bombarded with the immediate crises. I have included sample forms in the addendum at the back of the book. These forms will help you to see the big picture. You can easily create ledger sheets on your computer or just plain notebook paper. Feel free to modify them to your situation. We have successfully used these and similar forms in our counseling and are pleased to share them with you.

More than likely, especially during your first year, you will find it necessary to revise the life financial plan many times to eliminate debt. Your first edition of the life financial plan will show where your expenses are out of control. You will use the information in the first edition to begin making expense adjustments.

In extreme financial debt situations, it may be necessary to:

🔑 Develop a survival life financial plan.

This plan requires a major adjustment in your standard of living! It usually is short term, three to six months in length, but could extend longer depending upon your situation. It only covers essentials such as food, housing, transportation, utilities, and medical. It must be flexible and can be adjusted monthly as needed.

Ann and I started with the survival plan for the first six months. We made the decision not to go out to eat, not to buy any clothes, and to put every extra dime we made from picking up cans and any other odd job we could do to earn extra income minus our tithe toward our debt. Likewise, many I have counseled required the survival plan for a short period of time.

The survival life plan allows you to focus on the major basic needs. The other bills are still there, but as the saying goes, "You can't get blood out of a turnip." It's not an excuse to just forget these bills, but it allows you time to make wise decisions of how to pay bills that are not basic life needs. Later in this chapter, I will discuss additional keys that will apply to the implementation of the survival life financial plan.

🔑 Once you have control of your spending for basic needs, you will create new life financial plans implementing adjustments that address bills in arrears.

You must be diligent and committed in making wise spending decisions for basic needs. Become extremely frugal, even with basic needs. You need to eat, but do you buy a name brand item or a store brand? You need electricity, but can you adjust the thermostat two degrees to reduce power consumption? There are many ways to reduce expenses for basic needs, allowing additional money to allocate funds for other expenses. You can't procrastinate for an extended period to address any expenses beyond basic needs. You made these bills, and you must pay them or at least something on them as quickly as possible. We will address later how to acquire additional funds for these other expenses.

🔑 Once all bills are current, you will continue to create new life financial plans to eliminate all debts.

One young couple I counseled probably changed their life financial plan every month for the next year to accomplish their goal in getting out of debt. They were aggressive to monitor their spending and made sure every extra dollar was allocated toward a debt. The more aggressive you are, the sooner you will see debt melt away. I believe because of their faithfulness and aggressiveness, God intervened and allowed additional financial resources during the process to assist them and to give them a wow experience. God can do the same for you! We will address keys later in this chapter for eliminating each debt.

🔑 Once all debt is eliminated except your mortgage, you can then consider creating a standard life financial plan.

This standard plan not only includes your current income and basic needs expenses but also prepares you for life circumstances, non essentials (such as cable, satellite, cell phones, etc.), additional savings, retirement, wants (new vehicles, vacations, etc., but only after debts are dismissed).

The standard life plan is more flexible. It can change occasionally as income and needs arise. You will fill out every applicable category listed on the forms for a modest lifestyle.

I know this sounds like it could take a lifetime to develop, but I remind you it only took fourteen months for Ann and me to become debt-free with the exception of our mortgage. And we paid off a twenty-year mortgage loan in only six and a half years by implementing these same keys.

These plans do require commitment and sacrifice. However, the short term sacrifices and long term disciplines are well worth the benefits of being debt-free. God will give you the same wisdom and grace to become and stay debt free if you are committed, disciplined, and obedient.

It's one thing to have a life financial plan, but you must be accountable. Therefore, you must:

🔑 Continue to track expenses and income.

You do this by using allocation sheets and expense sheets. We have included examples of these forms in the addendum. Also, use a receipt file box organized by category to store receipts for quick reference. Organization will make documentation much easier and less time consuming.

It is important for you (and your spouse if you are married) to set up a time on a regular basis to document and review the financial records to assure you are following the life financial plan. This should happen weekly for the first few months progressing to monthly as financial life plans are revised toward a standard plan. I even suggest you sit down with any children that are at least ten years old and let them help you. It is good training for them and most likely will discipline them from asking for things they clearly see you can't afford. There are additional keys that also apply toward developing life financial plans. They are:

🔑 To become debt-free, you must have a plan!

All of us have dreams of things we desire to do and acquire. However, unless we develop a plan and implement it and become accountable, we probably will never achieve what we desire. It sums up to this: failing to plan is planning to fail and failing to account is also planning to fail. God has a plan for our life. He has placed it into action, and he holds us accountable. Why should we do any less for ourselves?

The goal of a life financial plan must be to eliminate unnecessary expenses and show were to sacrifice in order to achieve at minimum a balance between net income and expenses and, eventually, surplus income. It is important that you and your spouse must agree on the goals and sacrifices of the life financial plan. Men, I can tell you that if you sit down by yourself and develop a life plan, your wife will not be on board, and it will cause you additional problems in the future. Remember, by God's law your spouse and you are one, and two heads in unity are better than one. It is wise to learn the principle of oneness that Jesus taught!

> And Jesus knew their thoughts, and said unto them, Every kingdom divided against itself is brought to desolation;

and every city or house divided against itself shall not stand:

> Matthew 12:25 (KJV)

🔑 Spend by the life financial plan and not your bank account.

This is an important key to remain debt-free! It is too easy and misleading to simply look at your bank accounts. Although you must know the balances of your bank accounts and cash on hand, it is prudent to realize this money has been designated for debt reduction. The only safe method for spending is to have a balanced life financial plan for each expense and stick to the designated amounts for each category of expenses. Spending from the bank accounts could easily put you in a position of borrowing designated funds from one account to pay another. Eventually, the expense from the account you borrowed from will come due and then you have a financial crises in the making.

🔑 Set up a defense parameter.

Life circumstances are going to happen. Your car is going to have mechanical problems as will you appliances. Your furniture is not going to last forever. Your house will require maintenance. We are not the Israelites in the desert—your clothes are not going to last forty years. The odds are, sometime in your lifetime, you will get sick or develop a disease or a disability. Today, it is difficult to walk out of a hospital for less than $5,000! Stay a few days and have minor surgery and you could easily accumulate a hospital bill of $30,000 to $50,000. Have major heart surgery and the bill could easily increase to $100,000 plus. Failing to prepare for life circumstances isn't just plain foolishness; it is planning for financial disaster.

Setting up a defense parameter includes:

🔑 Developing multiple savings accounts.

> Go to the ant, thou sluggard; consider her ways, and be wise: Which having no guide, overseer, or ruler, Provideth her meat in the summer, and gathereth her food in the harvest.
>
> Proverbs 6:6–8 (KJV)

People often look at me and say, "Are you crazy? I can't pay my bills, and you are telling me to set up a savings account?" I can tell you that you are planning to fail unless you fund a savings account! To fund a savings account will require some immediate sacrifices. It may require doing things you don't desire to do. This discipline will test your obedience and your commitment to get out of debt and stay out of debt.

If ants gather during the harvest and store for times of no harvest, then surely you are as smart as ants. You simply can't consume all your income as you acquire it. You must put a portion of it aside for a day of no harvest. That day of no harvest comes for each of us.

I recommend having several savings accounts. Having more than one savings account will help you discipline yourself for various type bills.

🔑 Develop a survival emergency savings account.

In the beginning, this is the most important account to prepare for life circumstances and it will continue as part of your life financial plan.

You will need to *immediately* acquire $1,000 for this account. Later you will increase this amount! This account will be used to pay for small life circumstances that will arise during your process of getting out of debt. How can you acquire funds to set up this savings account? Go to your storage areas (your closets, attics, garages, and storage buildings) and any item you can absolutely do without, sell whatever it takes to raise the $1,000. This account will most likely take care of those unscheduled circumstances that will happen like the dryer breaking, minor repairs to the car or house, or an emergency visit to the doctor for a sickness or injury. In this day and time, medical cost to go to a doctor or maintenance cost can put a tremendous financial strain on a family's financial situation. You may be saying this is foolish but which is more foolish? Being head over heels in debt? Or selling everything you can possibly sell and making a temporary sacrifice to get out of debt? Even as I write this book, there have been recent situations where I had to evaluate what I owned and sell off items to pay an unplanned bill that was beyond my emergency savings.

Once you reach your goal of $1,000 in the survival emergency savings account, begin using any acquired extra money for paying off debts. Initially, continue to replenish this fund as emergencies draw down on the fund by additional sacrifices from your possessions. Later, after paying off debts, you will gradually increase the amount of your survival emergency fund savings account to a minimum of three months and a maximum of six months of actual living expenses from distribution of net income from the life financial plan. Remember, this is a special emergency saving account to be used only for unplanned emergencies. Increasing it to three to six months will also allow for basic living expenses if there is a temporary loss of income. This savings account is not for buying new TVs or the latest gadget. It is for emergencies only and for those basic needs that you can't do without.

In addition, I recommended you to do this:

🔑 Open an escrow savings account.

This savings account will be used for bills that occur over thirty days such as vehicle and property (house) insurance and vehicle and property taxes. It can also be used for bills occurring monthly, quarterly, or semi- annually with a surcharge to avoid the surcharges. This account will be funded from income distribution on your monthly life financial plan.

It is often those big, known tax and insurance bills you know are coming but fail to plan for that will create financial crises. If your loan institution doesn't escrow taxes and insurance or you have other bills that occur over thirty days, set up an escrow savings account. Simply divide the number of weeks before the bill is due and set aside that amount of money from your income into this account to cover these bills. Not only will you have the security of the money in the bank to pay the bill, but often, you can make lump sum payments on bills such as auto insurance and save any surcharges. A dollar saved is a dollar earned that can be used to get out of debt and stay out of debt. Once you have gotten through the first year, you then have a full twelve months or six months before the bill comes due giving you more available weekly funds to get out of debt. Keeping money intended for these bills in your checking account can be planning for failure. Quick glances at your checking account without reviewing your entire financial plan can deceive you into making bad decisions.

I also recommend after you have achieved three to six months savings in your emergency savings account to do the following:

🔑 Open a life circumstance savings account.

This savings account is for those circumstances that will occur during your lifetime such as housing, appliance, and auto repairs/replacements, vacation/special trips, special giving or gifts, and advanced education.

Life circumstances are going to happen. Your clothes are not going to last forty years, and it would be foolish not to lay aside money to replace them. Your car may last fifteen to twenty years, but it is going to require extensive repairs, and eventually you will have to replace it. Your appliances likewise will need repairs and replacement.

In all my years of doing handyman work, I know there is continual maintenance on your house. Regardless of the claims made by the paint manufacturers, I find if you don't paint your house, especially the doors and windows every two to three years, you will have rot. More than likely, you will also desire to make renovations to your present dwelling or even build or purchase a bigger home.

You are going to incur expenses when your kids go off to college or when they get married. There may be a death in your family that requires you to help or pay funeral or miscellaneous expenses related to the death.

You will be taking a vacation or taking special family trips that will add expenses. When you sit down and realize these things are going to happen, it is very foolish to wait until it is upon you to try to accumulate the needed funds. Planning for the future is very much biblical! Just remember that everything is to be done in moderation; otherwise, you could be guilty of hoarding and failing to trust in God's provisions.

If you never discipline yourself to accumulate funds in this life, circumstance savings account, you will be living from paycheck to paycheck, living a life of stress, unless you make more money than you spend.

My final recommendation for multiple savings accounts is to do the following:

🗝 Develop a retirement savings account.

This is an area you can't afford to neglect. Social Security is not going to completely fund your retirement. Retirement savings must become a priority right after the life circumstance savings account! But first, get out of debt! I remind you to be prudent in the life circumstance account and not to hoard.

You might even desire to split your savings between the life savings and the retirement savings to ensure both are properly funded. Funding for this account can also be multiplied by using programs offered by many businesses. Many employers offer tax qualified matched retirement accounts you should take advantage of. Their contribution is free money so grab it. I recommend you use pretax dollars to fund your account. You are drawing interest or investment increase potential on the total sum of the contribution with pretax contributions rather than on a smaller after tax contribution. You will eventually pay tax, but most likely at retirement you will be withdrawing monthly incremental amounts that will keep you in a lower tax bracket.

Warning: I learned the hard way it can be a tax nightmare receiving retirement distributions by partially funding a retirement account with both pretax and after tax contributions. Do only one or the other! If you do have a retirement plan that has both pretax and after tax dollars and desire to roll it into another plan, make sure the plan will continue to track the after tax dollars. Otherwise, you may find yourself paying taxes again on the after tax distributions. Consult with a CPA prior to rolling over retirement plans that have both in the same account.

It may be that you already have one of the tax qualified plans in place with your employer, but remember the first goal is to get out of debt to free up more funds. I have advised some successfully to reduce the amount of contribution to their qualified plans until they are out of debt and then restore the amount of reduction from their pay checks or even add more. I will talk about retirement more in chapter seven.

Start as early as possible preparing for retirement. If you are already older than forty-five, you will have to be very aggressive to properly fund your retirement. I would recommend you take all you documents to a Christian financial advisor and let them help you develop a retirement savings account. Again, your first priority is to get out of debt to free up money. Then you can use the available money to plan for your future.

What is the best way to fund these multiple savings accounts through your life financial plan?

🔑 Develop an eighty-twenty life financial plan.

A good starting rule for savings is what I call the eighty-twenty plan. Start saving with a maximum of 80 percent of your net income going toward living expenses, a minimum of 10 percent for tithes, and 10 percent for savings. As you decrease your living expenses, you can simply modify the life financial plan ratio and increase giving and savings.

Another key I immediately put into practice is this:

🔑 Commit future wage increases to savings.

This requires you to keep your standard of living the same regardless of any wage increases. This was one of the first keys I put into practice once I was debt-free with the exception of my mortgage. For a period of ten years, I split nearly every wage increase between a bank savings account and my employer matched retirement investment program. The third, sixth, and ninth years, I received the wage increase to offset inflation. Those small accumulative raises add up to more than you can imagine especially if you invest them wisely.

🔑 Communicate with your creditors.

If you are in a serious financial crisis, don't keep your creditors in the dark. Talk to them! You will find in some situations they will assist you through this difficult time.

🔑 Don't ignore the debt!

I can't stress how important this is! Inform all creditors of your situation in writing and/or in person. If possible, send creditors at least five dollars each month as a good faith effort to say, "I'm trying!"

In addition, give the creditors a copy of your life financial plan (budget). This allows them to see your financial capabilities. And ask for Hardship Assistance. Sometimes, if you do this, they will reduce the interest rate, or, sometimes, they will allow you to pay interest only, and/or sometimes, they will simply give forgiveness of the debt.

After implementing these keys for some I have counseled, I have personally seen a seventeen-thousand-dollar debt forgiven at a bank. I have seen three hundred thousand plus in medical debts forgiven by medical institutions and providers. In other situations, payments and interest were reduced considerably during the hardship period. Although I have had a few bank card companies forgive debt, as a general rule, bank cards are not as forgiving, but we have had some success in forgiveness or reduction of interest. Let me warn you that you are going to receive intimidating calls from some companies. These call operators are trained to unnerve you so they can get you to make a financial commitment. But keep your cool and—

🔑 Commit only what you can actually fulfill.

Commit only according to your life financial plan availability of funds. Later, I will give you keys for paying off each creditor. The next important key is that you must do the following:

🔑 Maintain your priorities.

Priority number 1 is to God. Pay your tithes and give offerings as prompted by God. You want God's favor, and Malachi 3 is clear that when you honor God, he will bless you; and when you withhold from God, you are cursed.

Priority number 2 is absolute need. Food, housing, medical, transportation—this means you can't live in the best, drive the biggest, and eat out several times a week and not pay your bills. Make the necessary sacrifices now to enjoy more of the finer things later.

Priority number 3 is to treat your creditors fairly. Pay each creditor something each month with any available funds you may have. Do it by the percentage of the creditor's minimum monthly payment against the total sum of all creditors' monthly minimum payments.

Again, be careful not to make further commitments you can't keep without withholding from other creditors. Try to make minimum payments, but if five dollars is all you can rightfully send, don't commit to twenty-five dollars.

The next session I want to introduce, I call "digging for gold." This is simply looking for ways to find more available resources or funds that you can apply toward getting out of debt. It also requires that you do the following:

🔑 **Change your attitude and behaviors.**

We have already addressed this key in previous sessions, but it is such an essential element of getting out of debt that it is worth being repeated. Fasting and praying is essential for changing our attitude which results in discipline and accountability.

🔑 **Commit to maintaining a simple lifestyle regardless of any income increases.**

Use any raises, gifts and refunds, minus tithe to pay off existing debt and for increasing savings and retirement account balances. I did this, and when my second layoff came, I had saved $27,000 which helped us to survive the next two years. Because I was a professional without a degree, I could not get a job doing what I was trained to do, and because I had been a professional for five years, I couldn't get a laborer's job because employers thought I didn't know how to do physical labor anymore. By necessity, I returned to the trade of construction I had taken in high school and survived.

Now let's look at some practical ways to find useable income to get out of debt.

🔑 Reduce and eliminate current spending.

Entertainment and recreation may be a large percentage of your monthly expenses. Make fewer or no trips to the movies, ball games, video stores, golf outings, etc., and it will add additional money to pay toward debt reduction.

In today's technological age, we believe cell phones, cable or satellite TV, and Internet services are a must-have. Reduce to lower plans or eliminate them entirely rather than sacrificing real needs. The argument I hear all the time against elimination of cell phones is "I will have to pay a penalty to eliminate." However, it's simple math: Compare the months remaining on the contract verses the penalty and choose the cheaper. Usually, it is cheaper to pay the penalty!

Eliminate home phone perks such as call waiting, voice mail, etc. You may even need to eliminate the home phone entirely for at least a season.

When tracking expenses people often find miscellaneous spending is a category they spend far more than they realized. Gifts are usually the largest single expense. Make gifts, and/or inform family of your financial crises and let them know you can't afford gifts at this time. I remember going to my brother-in-law and telling him we couldn't afford to buy Christmas gifts for all the family (it wasn't easy). His response was, "We really can't afford to give all the family gifts either."

Now we can have Christmas as a family and really enjoy being together without the added dread of searching for just the right gifts and the expense of buying them. As for miscellaneous spending, I made a practice of not carrying more than $2 in my wallet at any time, and not buying what I really don't need.

You can save on your utilities expenses. Turn off lights when you leave the room. Set thermostats at lower temperatures in the winter and higher in the summer to reduce run time. You can always dress in the house to be warmer or cooler. Unplug appliances when they are not in use. Most modern appliances use power even when they are turned off.

Car washes, lawn care, car and home maintenance are expenses that can be reduced or eliminated. Do it yourself to save money! There is plenty of how-to information on the Internet. Your health could benefit from the physical and mental labors required to perform the task.

Eliminate or reduce the times you go to restaurants. The average family can prepare seven to eight meals at home for the price of eating out one meal.

I have counseled families where the husband was wearing expensive rings, and the wife had thousands of dollars of necklaces around her neck, expensive earrings on and multiple finger rings, yet they were in financial trouble and didn't know what to do. Have you thought that you may be wearing part of the answer to your financial situation? Satan can blind you so that you can't see the simple things to do to get out of debt. Look for the obvious things. No matter how small, it can put you on a path of becoming debt-free. Sell these items and use the money to get out of debt! Sacrifice today to be blessed tomorrow.

I'm not against pets, but it is very simple. If you can't pay your bills, you can't afford pets. Are you going to feed, clothe, and shelter your children or your pets?

Addictions are expensive. Sadly, I find many needy and poor individuals are in bondage with addictions. Addictions are a spiritual problem, and many people need spiritual assistance and the right motivation to get free of them. My father smoked unfiltered Camel cigarettes and half and half pipe tobacco for forty-one years. He tried everything on the market to quit. I personally know about the affects of secondhand smoke. I have battled with bronchitis or pneumonia at least once a year for most of my life because the doctors say my lungs were damaged as a child from breathing secondhand smoke. One day, while visiting my dad, I told him, "Dad, I love you greatly and want to be around you, but when you smoke around me, it is like someone putting a knife in my chest." Two months later, he called me and told me he had stopped smoking without any market products. All he needed was the right motivation. He loved me dearly, wanted to see me and didn't want to cause me pain! In other situations, I have seen people go to an altar intoxicated and rise sober with their eyes clear and no smell of alcohol on them; or when in bondage with tobacco products, they rise free from that bondage. Many Christians working with people with the addition of various drugs have had similar experiences. I'm saying that you can be free from addictions!

You are the temple of God according to God's word. Would you deface or purposely damage a church building? I don't think most people would even consider damaging a church building, and you are so much greater than any building of brick and wood!

Paul said,

> Know ye not that ye are the temple of God, and that the Spirit of God dwelleth in you? If any man defile the temple of God, him shall God destroy; for the temple of God is holy, which temple ye are.
>
> 1 Corinthians 3:16–17 (KJV)

Christians, you are a holy vessel unto the Lord. We see in the Old Testament where God established his temple to be respected and not desecrated. Death was the penalty for defiling the temple. Under grace, God didn't change his judgment concerning defilement. When you abuse your body, whether it is overeating, with tobacco products, alcohol or illegal drugs, there is judgment. Look at the diseases and death rate attributed to these addictive habits. Look at the enormous cost to support these habits. Freedom from these addictions will free up money to set you free from the bondage of debt.

I'm not against using market products to assist you in breaking a habit, and there are a lot of good organizations that will help you. But foremost, you need the right motivation and spiritual assistance to break additions.

I have also found through my counseling that people who can least afford to waste money are the ones most likely to struggle over giving up cell phones, house phones, internet, cable or satellite TVs. They also are the ones who justify eating out. Still, it is plain and simple: if you can't afford these items, it is foolish to keep them or continue doing them. They will only drag you further down. It's better to eat at home than to talk on a phone or play golf or check out the newest restaurant. Sell the bass boat, and pay your rent or mortgage so you have a roof over your head. Take that movie or eating out money and pay your rent. If you are not ready to give up these items to get out of debt, then you are not serious about getting out of debt. Remember, the sacrifice is for a season, and you can restore all these things and pay cash to replace them once you are out of debt.

Eliminating or reducing all of the above expenses will immediately give you extra money to reduce your debt. Get that debt monkey off your back!

Again, I remind you how Ann and I did the extreme. We decided that we would not go out to eat, buy clothes, or spend on entertainment until we got everything paid off except the house mortgage. Fourteen months later, we were completely out of debt except for our house, and six and a half years later, our house was paid for. We did restore many of the small things we sacrificed shortly after the fourteen months passed. I can tell you it was worth it to get out from under the bondage of debt.

Let's address some additional ways you can acquire money to pay down your debts.

🔑 Make income tax adjustments.

I have counseled with people who get tax refunds of $4,000 or more every year and are head over heels in debt. This is plain foolishness! I've had people tell me this is the only way they can save money! Because you lack discipline, you are going to allow the government to accumulate $4,000 of your money and not pay you one cent of interest for fifteen to eighteen months? "Pay the money to me, and I'll make interest on your money for me"—this is not even good common sense. I, too, had trouble disciplining myself to save money at first, so I got with my employer and had them to deduct a certain amount of money each week and deposit it in a bank in another city. Having the savings in another city made it harder for me to leisurely drop by the bank and withdraw the funds. It worked! Now, I have developed the disciplines and can keep it in my local bank. You can simply avoid over paying your taxes by:

🔑 Changing your W-9 withholding allowance.

Simply divide your refund by fifty-two weeks and find the nearest withholding allowance to that amount. Take the difference each week in pay minus the tithe and put some of it in savings and pay the balance on a debt. So what if you owe the government at the end of the year. You have saved the money and gained interest. Just pay the IRS what you owe!

🔑 Bargain shop.

Use coupons when you shop! The internet and newspapers are great resources for coupons! There are people who can teach you how to buy hundreds of dollars of groceries for a few dollars. If you really work coupons, you can get a lot of grocery items free. Caution: Don't hoard! That is unscriptural! Learn from those that help others with the surplus. You can bless other families greatly without it costing you one cent. Many charitable organizations will gladly accept your surplus to help the poor and needy.

Shop only during sales, but only buy what you need unless you are securing free merchandise to give away!

Closets can hang full of bargain clothes, as well as food pantries and freezers. But it really is not a deal unless you use it. I have been to yard sales with the original retail tag still attached to the garments. I have seen food thrown away because it was too old and freezer burnt to eat. This is like money thrown in the wind.

You can get great deals at Goodwill, Salvation Army, and/or other thrift stores.

Ann is a great shopper! She knows how, when, and where to find deals. She generally pays less than 25 percent of retail prices for clothes at major retail stores. Her outfits purchased at major retail stores usually cost less than $20. As for me, my suits usually cost me $10 at Goodwill, and Ann always saves on my shoes often buying one pair at a reduced price and getting the second pair for free. She also gets great deals on my shirts and pants.

Another way to find additional resources is by doing the following:

🔑 Refinancing your home.

You will save on the total interest paid. You will reduce monthly mortgage payments. However, if possible, I recommend you continue to make the same previous monthly payment amount, and you will automatically reduce the months owed on the mortgage. Ann and I did this as well and added any extra money we could accumulate and paid a twenty-year mortgage off in six and one half years.

Another way to find additional resources is by doing the following:

🔑 Reclaiming the escrow on your home.

I don't mean *taking out* an equity loan against your home. I'm not a fan of risking your home to pay off secured or unsecured debts. Rather than an equity loan, *sell* your home and secure any escrow. If your debt situation is so serious that you are struggling to make the payments and are constantly late, then it's time to downsize—especially if you lose your job put your house on the market for sale. Don't wait until you receive a notice from the creditor of intent to foreclose. Sell the house as quickly as possible and use any equity toward securing a place you can afford and to pay off your debts. It's foolish to hold onto a house you can't afford and then also lose any equity you have in it. This happens a lot! Be a wise steward!

Another way to find additional financial resources is to do the following:

🔑 Modify auto and home insurance.

You can increase deductibles and save hundreds of dollars. Eliminate perks such as towing, medical, rental, underinsured motorist coverage, and even change the amount of coverage for uninsured coverage. A $2 savings is $2 you will have available to put on a debt. Self-insure to absorb as much liability as you can afford.

Auto and home insurance is usually one area most people don't even consider when trying to reduce their expenses. You can often save money without changing companies! My eldest son followed my advice and saved over $400 with the same company while insuring two vehicles. Shop around for the best premiums. I have found age can play a big role in auto insurance premiums. As stated previously, *self-insure* yourself as much as possible. I have made it a rule that when my vehicle trade-in value drops to $5,000, I only carry a fifty-one hundred-fifty liability and/or whatever is required by law for uninsured protection. This will cover most vehicles if I'm involved in an accident. I figure that if I lose my vehicle, I can survive the loss.

Have you noticed today's television ads where nearly every auto insurance company is promising $300 plus savings over their competitors' quotes? How can that be? Get the real story and compare before you buy insurance!

Simply increasing your deductable on your home policy will reduce your premiums. Talk with your agent about reducing or eliminating unnecessary perks.

🔑 Increase health insurance deductibles and co-pays.

You need to protect your family. In this day you can't afford health insurance, but you can't afford to be without it. You can financially survive with some doctor bills, but can you financially survive a $50,000 or $100,000 hospital bill? Usually the best buys for health insurance is through your employer plans as your employer is probably paying 25% or more of the premium. However, in an effort to reduce cost, many small employers are eliminating health insurance plans. Regardless, you need some type of health insurance or coverage to assist you with those major bills. In the summer of 2012 the new health care law was declared constitutional by the Supreme Court and requires everyone to purchase health insurance by 2014 or pay a tax penalty. There are some exemptions to this requirement to purchase health insurance.

If you are a Christian, there are several non-profit associations you can join and be exempt from this law. Christian Care Medi-Share is one of the organizations which is *not* insurance, but it is Christians in an association helping each other with their medical bills. Ann and I have belonged to Christian Care Medi-

Share since 2001, and it has been not only a blessing because the premiums are lower than insurance, but the support staff shows real care and compassion for the members. Also, I like the idea of paying my money directly to fellow members' medical bills rather than making some executives at some large insurance firm rich. You can find this non-profit organization and others on the internet. They do require a lifestyle of healthy living to join. I have no vested interest in this company other than being a satisfied customer.

If you don't desire to get involved in these associations, at least sacrifice for the following:

🔑 Purchase a major medical plan.

Major medical plans only cover hospital expenses. They are much cheaper than a comprehensive medical plan. They may have a $2,500 or more deductable, but it sure beats owing $50,000 or more in medical bills.

You can also do what follows:

🔑 Set up a pretax health maintenance account.

These accounts are only available if you have a large deductible. However, they have great benefits for using the funds in the account to pay your deductibles and co-pays. They can be set up with banks or insurance companies. I will discuss this more in chapter six.

🔑 Purchase the right life insurance.

Again, you have a responsibility to protect your family, but you also have a mandate to be a wise steward. In chapter six, I will talk more about buying insurance, but I'm going to give you two rules to follow that are prudent for buying insurance.

🔑 Buy insurance according to you liabilities.

You determine your liabilities by asking these questions: If I die, what bills would my spouse have? What would be the cost of child care and schooling for any children I may have? And how much could my spouse earn to offset these expenses? Life Insurance should not be designed to make your spouse rich, but it should be enough to make sure the liabilities are met.

Now, I'm going to get myself in trouble with insurance agents with my next statement, but I sold insurance for about eight years and often sold the wrong type policy because of a lack of knowledge.

🔑 Buy term insurance.

Preferably, a twenty-year-level term policy! Term insurance is the best deal for the money! Term insurance is cheaper than whole life and the many variations of whole life! This type policy will get your children to adulthood, give you time to prepare to be self-insured, and give you time to get out of debt! Know this: if the policy accumulates dividends, you are paying too much for the insurance. Find a good twenty-year term policy and take the difference in premium and invest it in a mutual fund or even an annuity. Reminder: Pay off your debts first with the savings! If for some reason you need large coverage for a short term, buy an annual renewable term policy. They are extremely cheap especially for young men and women.

Remember this important key:

🔑 Insurance is for liabilities you can't afford.

Buying large insurance policies just to profit off the death of someone reveals the spiritual problem of greed and a spiritual problem of not trusting God!

Now that I may have ruffled some feathers, let's move to the next keys for acquiring additional funds:

🔑 Liquidate to eliminate.

Here is the rule: what helped get you in debt will help get you out of debt.

Can't eat it, sleep on it, or drive it, get rid of it! We seemingly love to hold on to our things whether we use them or not. But things as a general rule can be replaced. If you are serious about getting out of debt, this is a minor sacrifice. Sell off anything you absolutely can live without, and put the money against your debts. You can advertise on eBay, craigslist, or in the newspapers. You can have yard and garage sales. You can also sell at the local auctions or go to the local pawn shops. Small dollars add up when you are trying to eliminate debt.

I counseled one lady who was three months behind on her house payment, had maxed out all her credit cards, and had borrowed all she could from family and friends. She had just bought a brand new TV that cost $1,000. I told her to sell it. Her argument was that she still owed money on it, and she could only get about $500 if she sold it. My response, "Is it not easier to pay off $500 than $1,000? When you get out of debt, you can save the money and go pay cash for a new TV." This is only common sense! Our forefathers knew and practiced this principle to survive. Even since Ann and I got out of debt, situations have occurred where my savings couldn't handle the total expense, and it required me to sell off something to pay the bill. Usually, I found the item I sold was a convenience that I could easily live without.

🔑 Accumulate to eliminate.

Ways to accumulate additional income:

Be responsible with raises. This was a promise I made to God, and God blessed me. He has also blessed others who have made this commitment. It is important that you don't change your standard of living because you get a raise. Apply this blessing to your debt and later to savings when you are debt-free. Even after I got out of debt, for the next five years, I invested my raises instead of changing my standard of living. In this way, God prepared me financially for my final layoff from a high paying job.

Get a second job. Acquiring a second job will speed up the process of becoming debt free as long as you apply all the income minus expenses toward debt, and maintain the disciplined lifestyle.

Spouse gets temporary job in the market place. I say temporarily because it is more important in the long term for the wife to remain at home to nurture the children and to support her husband. It is the role of the husband where possible to financially support his family.

Older children may get jobs to contribute. I started working on a farm at the age of six, and the money I made went to pay for my clothes. If you have a teenager, they can work summer or weekend jobs to help support the family. Explain to them the need, and allow them to keep a portion of their earnings.

Use financial gifts from family and friends to pay off debts instead of purchasing additional items.

We have given you some ways to acquire additional income to get that debt monkey off your back. God can open more doors when he see's your commitment and disciplines. Make sure you apply any additional income minus tithes to dismiss debt!

The last practical key I'm going to share with you in this chapter is this:

🗝 Tear down that debt mountain!

There are other writers who call this plan by different names. But it simply is God's plan! It is what he gave me and to others during financial crises. Right now, your debt may look like a mountain that can't be destroyed! How do you tear down a mountain? The answer is one stone at a time! Likewise, a debt mountain is removed one debt at a time. You will simply treat each debt as its own mountain. You will start by tearing down the smallest mountain first, then move to the next and so forth until every mountain has been eliminated. You will then be debt-free!

Some would advise putting a little extra money on each debt or choosing the debt that has the highest interest rate and paying any extra money on it. This seems reasonable, but with either of these plans, I find they often fail. Why? Because if your debt is enormous after using these methods, you will most likely still owe most if not every one of the creditors a year later and will feel like you have not accomplished anything. I have found everyone needs encouragement and a sense of accomplishment. The plan God gave me gives the needed encouragement when you see the number of debts decreasing in a shorter period of time and accomplishes the goal of becoming debt free quicker. But remember, it is important to do the following:

🔑 Make minimum monthly payment on all accounts.

Sometimes, even this is not possible. You may only have five dollars extra a month to pay on the debt rather than the minimum required. If this is the case, be sure to talk to your creditors and show them a plan of how you will eventually pay them. Now, let's start tearing down debt mountains!

🔑 Attack the smallest debt first!

Put as much extra money as possible on the smallest account. Don't worry about the interest rate right now. Your goal is to eliminate the smallest debt as quickly as possible. Immediately use any extra funds you acquired by applying the reducing, liquidation, and accumulating keys to pay off this debt or greatly reduce it. Often, you can immediately eliminate your smallest bill. If not, use any extra monthly life financial plan funds acquired by applying the reducing, liquidation, and accumulating keys and increase the monthly payment. Again, be sure to pay the minimum on all other accounts. Let's say you only found $20 extra money each month after applying the previous keys. The smallest debt has a $15 minimum monthly payment so instead of making a $15 payment each month you make a $35 payment until it is paid off. You will be surprised at how quickly the balance reaches zero.

Once this debt is paid, attack the next smallest debt by adding the previous debt payment to the minimum balance. Continue using this same process until every single debt is paid!

By putting this plan into action, you will find the debts will go away very quickly. Once you have paid off the last smaller debt, then attack the mortgage debt with this same key. You could find that you literally could be doubling your monthly mortgage payment, thus, cutting many years off the finance period and saving tens or hundreds of thousands of dollars.

What is the final result?

You are debt free! You now can have a savings account! You can buy new cars, new appliances, and furniture and pay cash. You can take vacations and pay cash! More importantly, you have available money that God can use to help others including your own family!

What you will experience on this journey of becoming debt-free will be amazing! You will see the impossible made possible. You may see money come from sources you didn't expect. You may receive free gifts. You may receive forgiveness of debts or interest rates reduced drastically. You may even find money as I did or find greater bargains on the goods you purchase. However, the greatest thing you will experience is freedom of the spirit to worship God as your relationship deepens.

Make this declaration: I will be debt free!
In the next chapter, I will address "buying with wisdom."
In closing, pray this prayer,

> Father, I thank you for all you have done for me and my family! I will take what you have taught me and apply it as I manage your possessions. Let me experience your mercy and power through my obedience and your grace. Give me a testimony to share with others for them also to be delivered from bondage. In Jesus's name, I pray. Amen.

BUYING WITH WISDOM

In this chapter, I will address some keys I have learned about buying items common to most every family. As always, I recommend you counsel with a Christian advisor who has extensive knowledge of the subjects before making major decisions.

🔑 Don't make hasty decisions.

One lesson I have learned through the years is to look for bargains. They are out there if you are willing to be patient and look for them. I've learned not to buy as soon as a gadget hits the market. The price will become lower if I'm patient to wait. I've learned what real deals are. I've learned that if it sounds too good to be true, it probably is not true. I've learned not to be hasty in my decisions. The biggest mistakes I have made were quick decisions. Salesmen hate to hear, "Thank you, but I don't buy big ticket items the same day I look at them."

> The thoughts of the diligent tend only to plenteousness;
> but of every one that is hasty only to want.
>
> Proverbs 21:5 (KJV)

🔑 Make knowledgeable decisions.

There are many things we may need in life, but many people are foolishly deceived into making purchases they cannot afford or are not right for their situation because of a lack of knowledge and understanding. I have learned to do the *research* and to get all the knowledge I can prior to making purchases. Sometimes, that means inquiring and getting the advice of someone who does have the knowledge I don't possess. God has a lot to say in his word about knowledge.

> The heart of the prudent getteth knowledge; and the ear of the wise seeketh knowledge.
>
> Proverbs 18:15 (KJV)

God surrounds me with godly men and women that care about me. These friends possess knowledge I often require to make good decisions. Likewise, God has surrounded you with knowledgeable people to help you make the right choices in life. The older I get, the more I miss the wisdom of my deceased grandparents and my father. As a young man, I didn't realize the storehouse of knowledge God had set before me.

> The hoary head is a crown of glory, if it be found in the way of righteousness.
>
> Proverbs 16:31 (KJV)

Swallow your pride and go to the elderly and ask for their wisdom. They have lived a long time and experienced many of the same situations you will encounter in life. Often, I look at my children and my friends' children and see the dangers of where they are headed because I have already walked a similar road. They often don't desire advice, but if only they would inquire, they would be so much better equipped to make better life decisions and avoid suffering from the consequences of bad decisions.

Like most people, I have made some bad purchases for one reason or another. Usually, those purchases were made mostly out of a lack of knowledge or ignorance. Now, Ann and I have the knowledge and understanding to share with you about buying specific items with wisdom.

PURCHASING OR REPLACING A CURRENT AUTO

We have all experienced the frustration of constant vehicle repairs. The immediate thought is to get rid of that junker and purchase a replacement vehicle. But is this wisdom? It could be, but only if you have crunched the numbers, done the proper research, and everything that correctly points to replacement. What is the real cost of the newer vehicle including interest if you finance? How many items are broke or not functioning properly? What is the cost to replace the major components of the old vehicle? How old is your current vehicle? When you list the pros and cons, put all this down on paper so you can make the best comparison.

People ask, "What is the cheapest car to own?"

🔑 Normally, the cheapest vehicle to own is the vehicle you presently own!

I was attending a financial seminar by the late Larry Burkett some years ago, and he made a statement which has stuck with me. Without quoting verbatim, he said that he drove his car until it turned to dust, and then he picked up the dust, compacted it, and drove it a while longer! Often, we get in a hurry to make a decision and miss out on what God desires to do for us. Personally, I don't even consider replacing my vehicle until it is twelve years old or has 250,000 miles on the engine. I'm able to do this because I don't let the little maintenance items accumulate. I normally fix them as they break. Allowing them to accumulate will only frustrate you and tempt you to make wrong choices. Eventually, you determine it is time to replace your vehicle, but before making a decision, you should:

🔑 Allow God the opportunity to provide for your needs according to his will.

Larry also told us he had been praying as he needed another vehicle. He had saved about $5,000 to replace his old vehicle, but God told him to give the money to someone in need. Just like you and me, he wrestled with this as he really needed a newer vehicle. But trusting God's wisdom, he gave the money to the needy person. Once he had obeyed God's instruction, someone immediately gave him a better vehicle than he would have been able to purchase. But the story didn't end with this one vehicle as within days, several more vehicles were given to him. He was able to use these vehicles to expand the ministry of his organization. This is just a sample of how God works when we get him involved in our decisions. Don't be surprised when God goes above and beyond your needs.

> I am come that they might have life, and that they might have it more abundantly.
>
> John 10:10 (KJV)

God's answers for your situation might be a gift vehicle, a great bargain, the right vehicle, or keep what you have, and I will give you grace.

Let's say you have done all your homework, you prayed and believe it God's desire for you to have a replacement vehicle. That leaves the question of whether you purchase a new or used vehicle. My recommendation:

🔑 Buy a used vehicle versus a new vehicle.

I bought my last new car around 1982. Since I didn't have the money to purchase it, I did like most everyone and secured a loan. The standard loan period was three years, and you could ask for a four year loan at a higher interest rate. Now the loan period can be six to seven years due to the high cost of new vehicles. The problem I have encountered in counseling is these extended loan periods can easily put you into a position of owing more money than the vehicle is worth. In the event you are in financial trouble, you may find you can't sell the car; and if it is repossessed, the bank or credit company will sell it at a far lesser value and you still have to make payments on a vehicle you no longer own. You know by now that I don't endorse debt, but if you feel you must borrow to get a vehicle, my rule of thumb is:

🔑 **If you can't easily make the four year payments, you are buying too much car for your income. Preferably you should use the three-year schedule or less.**

Everyone likes a new car, but is the price really worth it? Is it the best bargain?

I have heard reports stating the average new vehicle looses 60 percent to 70 percent of its value in the first four years. You can see by this way, you could easily owe more on a vehicle than its value. In my opinion based upon these calculations, new vehicles are never really a deal unless the dealer gives extreme discounts where the final retail price would be at least equal to fair trade in value of the previous year model. This is especially true if you have to finance it. (Note: I said fair trade in value! Don't look for this to happen unless the dealership is going out of business and is just clearing the lot!)

Warning: Be wary of all the TV commercials and newspaper advertisements. How can they give thousands of dollars in discounts and stay in business? Well, everything is based off manufacturer's suggested retail pricing. What is that? Where did it come from? Do you really believe those ads on TV where they advertise a gadget for $19.95? They then offer to give you two along with additional items to boot if you order within the next five minutes and just pay the additional shipping and handling. Then to top it off, they claim the value is $70 for only $19.95. Come on, let's get real! Those numbers are a number someone in marketing pulled out of the sky to make it sound like a great bargain. Likewise, the manufacturer's suggested retail price on vehicles is a number someone in marketing pulled out of the sky to ensure that when you finish haggling, the dealership can still make a sizeable profit. I can't image anyone going to a car dealership and paying the manufacturer's suggested retail price. We all know that is not the dealer's best selling price. When I was a young man, my father told me to always ask for more than I knew I would get for an item I wanted to sell to ensure I got the price I wanted. If you go to any third world country, they will expect you to negotiate the price down. Likewise, car dealerships know you will feel better about your purchase if you believe you saved thousands of dollars. Based upon my research, I have the opinion that new vehicles are not the bargain the dealerships make them out to be. Thus, I buy great used cars and save thousands of dollars.

Though I don't recommend you buy new cars, if you must then you should know the following keys:

🔑 Research prices on the internet and through your bank.

There are a lot of non-dealer web sites that will give you true values of vehicles. Most dealers will match other dealer's ads. Go to your local bank with all the information and they can also give you values of the vehicles.

🔑 Don't buy the first day you look at a vehicle.

You need time to digest the information and pray for discernment. If the car is not there later, then I believe it was not meant for you.

🔑 Offer trade-in value.

Did you know the moment you drive a vehicle off the lot, it will automatically loose approximately 10 percent of its value? It's considered a used vehicle! I had a family member that learned this lesson. Trade-in value in my opinion is the real value of the vehicle. They probably will not accept that price, but like the manufacturer's suggested retail price, it gives you a starting negotiation point.

🔑 The offered selling price today is good tomorrow.

Walk away from any salesman that tells you they will not give you the same price if you leave the lot and come back. It's probably not a deal anyway. It's a means to manipulate you. Do you really want to buy from a manipulator?

🔑 Negotiate on the phone.

Car salesmen are trained experts, they know how to get a commitment out of you. You are probably not going to win if you are on their turf. The last new car I bought over the phone, I had done my research and knew the maximum I would pay. I told the salesman I didn't have to buy a new car, and if they couldn't make money at the price I offered then I certainly understood. They called me every day for the next three days making a counter offer. On the third day, I purchased the car within $50 of my original offer.

🔑 Be patient! Don't call them, let them call you!

Make the educated offer and tell them you will immediately come in and buy the car at the price you offered. Automatically, they will make a counter offer. Be persistent and firm in your offer. If you know your offer is an educated offer and the dealer is persistent with their offer, then thank them but tell them it's not good enough and to call you if they change their minds. No matter how bad you may desire that vehicle, don't get impatient! Don't call them. It is a sign of your weakness that they will latch onto. Remember, the dealer is not going to lose money to make a sale, but if they really desire to sell you a car and they can make money, they will finally give you their rock bottom price. If you have done your research correctly, it will be at or extremely close to your original offer. If they don't call, contact another dealer.

🔑 Sell your vehicle instead of trading it.

You have better negotiating power if you don't trade in your old vehicle. Unless your old car is ready for the junk yard, you likely will be able to receive more money by selling it yourself. If it is junk then sell it to the junk yard. Most vehicles will bring between $150 and $400 at today's scrap metal prices. Again, don't fall for the gimmicks dealerships offer. How do you think they can offer you thousands of dollars more for your car than the car's book value? The only way would be because of the inflated manufacturer's suggested retail price on the new car. In many situations, you probably could have bought the new vehicle close to the same price without the over inflated trade value they offer. If you don't desire to personally sell your old vehicle then negotiate the lowest price first and then introduce you might be interested in a trade. Most likely, they will offer you lower than fair trade in value if they have really given you their rock bottom price. Insist on a minimum of fair trade in value, but start with at least good value in your negotiations. Forget excellent fair trade value as it seems to me even if you tried to trade in a brand new vehicle you would not get excellent fair trade value from a dealer. Again, I no longer buy new vehicles. I buy good used vehicles. I would buy a current year new vehicle if the dealership would sell it to me for the fair trade in value of the previous year model. However, I have never had that to happen so I continue to buy good used vehicles.

🗝 Used three- to four-year-old vehicles are the best value for the money!

The major depreciation is complete on a three or four year old vehicle. They are at realistic and affordable prices. Most minor defects have already been fixed. Manufacturer's warranties may still be good on at least the major components. I have had great success with used vehicles as I did my homework and entered the deals educated.

How and where to buy a used vehicle?

🔑 First choice is to buy directly from the dealer's wholesale auctions.

This is my preferred method of buying used vehicles. Use the same principles shown above for buying a new and used vehicle. Buying directly from a dealer's wholesale auction will require finding a small independent used vehicle dealer that knows what to look for, and you can trust who is willing to work with you to purchase the vehicle you desire. You will need to know just what you want and give them some parameters. More than twelve years ago, my daughter found such a dealer, and he has bought nearly all her and her husband's vehicles and all but one vehicle for Ann and me. Every vehicle he has purchased for us has been outstanding. He wants us for repeat business so he looks out for our interest. He has been in the business long enough to know all the gimmicks and tricks used to hid defects. There was a truck I wanted to buy, but after he inspected it, he would not buy it for me. He told me he would not sell it on his lot, and he would not buy it for me unless I insisted.

These dealers will usually charge you $300 to $400 above the dealer's auction price. Depending on the model, you can often purchase the vehicles for thousands of dollars below market value. They can do this because when they go to buy for you, they know it's a done deal. Their only expense is going to the auction and driving the car off the lot and filling out the documents. Our dealer bought a beautiful three year old truck without a scratch for $13,900 including his fee, the property tax, tags, sales tax, and title fee. I researched all the car lots in every city around checking prices, and the best price I could find to purchase a similar truck was about $18,000 not including the other fees.

🗝 **Second choice is to buy from an individual or new vehicle dealership.**

Again, use the same principles I shared for buying a new vehicle to buy a used vehicle. Your first offer should not exceed the fair market trade in value to new vehicle dealers. More than likely, they really paid hundreds of dollars less than this price. Don't be fooled if they show you documents of how much they gave in trade-in to the original owner. As stated previously, these figures are inflated to allure a person to buy the new vehicle. Your first offer to an individual selling their vehicle should not exceed $300 over fair trade, and your final offer should not exceed good trade in value. Always have your mechanic to check out the vehicle for needed repairs before you make the purchase from the new vehicle dealer or the individual. It may cost you $100, but it is well worth the expense. Walk away if the new vehicle dealer or the individual has a problem with you having your mechanic to check the vehicle. There probably are needed repairs they don't want you to know about.

Buying from a new car dealer is my second choice for securing a used vehicle. I don't usually buy used vehicles from new vehicle dealerships or individuals. The last time I bought a used car from a new vehicle car dealership, we bought it for the price we wanted. The car looked exceptional, but later we were very disappointed as signs started showing up the car had been in trouble. The problems appeared to be hidden by someone at a dealership somewhere as it was bought from a dealer's auction by the dealership. We failed to take the car to an independent mechanic to look over prior to buying. Lesson learned!

🗝 **Get preapproved at your financial institution if you are going to finance.**

I recommend financing with your local financial institution. You may get the same rate at the dealership as with your financial institution, but how the interest is calculated may mean you will pay more interest financing with the dealership. If you are going to buy directly from the dealer's auction through a used vehicle dealer, you will need to go to your bank or financial institution and get preapproved for a loan. You will need to authorize the bank to be prepared to immediately cut the dealer a check as soon as he provides the necessary documents.

Again, I'm convinced the best automobile buy is through an independent-used vehicle dealer that will contract for a fee to purchase you a vehicle at a dealer's auction. It requires some faith and a commitment to the dealer to buy you the best vehicle as generally only the dealer can look and possibly test drive the vehicles prior to purchase. However, my dealer has never bought my children or me a problem vehicle.

🗝 Pay cash for your replacement vehicle.

This should be your ultimate goal for replacing vehicles in the future. Paying cash requires purchasing vehicles you can really afford. Proper planning, using the sample life financial plan spreadsheet can make this key possible. Paying cash is really not difficult to do over a period of time. More than likely you are currently making vehicle payments.

🗝 You should make vehicle payments for the rest of your life!

But you should not be making payments to the finance institution. Make the payments to yourself! Here is how the plan works. Once you have paid off your debts (excluding your mortgage), set up a vehicle savings account and return to making the monthly vehicle payments amounts you previously made only deposit them into this vehicle savings account. You should be able to do this as you are now out of debt except for your mortgage. At least, deposit a large portion of the previous vehicle payment. The more you deposit, the quicker you will be able to replace vehicles and pay cash for them.

A $250 monthly savings over four years would give you $12,000 plus interest in the bank to purchase a replacement vehicle. No, you can't buy a new car with this amount, but you can buy a newer used car than you own. Be patient! By continuing to make car payments to yourself, you could potentially buy a brand new car and pay cash for it in less than twelve years. Don't forget the negotiation keys we discussed earlier.

LIFE INSURANCE

Review the information we provided on this subject in chapter 5. Insurance policies are like most bills passed by congress, the congressmen and even lawyers don't understand them fully. Likewise, the verbiage used in insurance documents is far above the average person's understanding including many insurance agents. The documents are often so difficult to comprehend we just take it for granted that the companies are going to do us right.

I think there is an important key we must be aware of concerning any legal contract whether it is a warranty, insurance policy, or any other type contract.

🔑 **The document always favors the seller over the buyer!**

As long as you understand the company is in business to make as much money as it can, you don't sign the document completely ignorant.

Everyone is told they need life insurance, but what you really need is to protect your family against liabilities in the event of your death! There is more than one way to protect against liabilities.

🔑 **Self-insure against liabilities.**

What are your liabilities? All your bills including continual expenses for such things as housing, food, clothing, medical cost, transportation, education, and burial expenses of you and your family are just some examples of liabilities. Your liabilities will change at various stages of your life. As children move out of your home or as you reduce debt, your liabilities should decrease. Therefore, you will need to be flexible insuring against liabilities. Your ultimate goal should be self insuring against liabilities. Life insurance is only one means of protection for your current liabilities.

🔑 **Savings and investments can do the same thing, and in my opinion, they are the better long term choices for liabilities protection!**

I'm not against insurance policies, but I believe they are misrepresented and grossly misused. Life insurance policies should only be a temporary tool to protect you and your family until you can self-insure against liabilities. Many major corporations self-insure themselves using insurance companies only to process claims. Why shouldn't individuals self-insure too? I realize most young couples don't have enough financial resources to protect themselves against most of their liabilities and will need a life insurance policy for the immediate liabilities. But I encourage you to begin planning to be self-insured as soon as possible. Hopefully, by the time your children reach adulthood you have prepared yourself financially for liabilities such as college and the children's marriage. Prior to reaching retirement, you should have savings to supplement any Social Security benefits and to cover burial expenses. With proper planning, you should not be in a financial position that requires you to purchase expensive guaranteed life insurance policies to cover burial liabilities in your senior years.

Sadly, I have counseled with many seniors that had not prepared for the death of a spouse and were grossly in debt. In the event that you have not prepared for death expenses, at least buy a guaranteed life policy that will take care of the burial expense. It's just plain wrong to leave this financial burden for your family after your death. Whether you are a young family or an unprepared senior, the option is to buy life insurance policies to cover the liabilities until you can save and invest to replace life insurance policies provisions.

Reminder: Your plan from the beginning should be toward becoming self-insured. However, it's *not* a plan. It's a dream unless you take *action* to make it happen. Everyone dreams. Sadly, few plan with action!

- **Purchasing burial plots, markers, vaults, caskets, and even paying for funerals in advance is an alternative method of protecting your family against death liabilities.**

There are two things certain in life. You are born, and you are going to die unless the Lord returns before your death takes place. Planning your funeral should be a natural undertaking. It takes away additional stress on the surviving spouse or children in having to make choices about the funeral arrangements and helps avoid making unwise choices based upon an emotional event. You and your spouse should meet with a funeral director and a cemetery director to start planning and acting upon preparing for death. Burial plots can be expensive if purchased in an emergency. Purchasing markers, vaults, and/or caskets at today's market price will be much cheaper than sometime in the future. Even if you are going to be cremated, you need to plan this in advance and consider options offered by the funeral home of your choice.

- **Pay cash for funeral arrangements!**

Paying cash today saves interest and cost increases. If you can't pay for everything at once, you can purchase funeral equipment and plans individually. Once you pay for one item then save for the next. Read the policies thoroughly and ask questions. Make sure all involved parties are in agreement and know the details and how to initiate the plans upon a death.

🔑 Protect your family only against liabilities which would be incurred at your death.

Often, the question is asked, "How much insurance do I need?" The amount will vary from person to person depending upon your liabilities. A young husband with small children in the home certainly has a greater liability than someone middle aged living alone. If you must buy life insurance, only buy enough to cover the liabilities your family will incur upon your death. I have heard the phrase insurance poor, and believe me, you can be if you try to make your family rich from your death. The following keys will help determine how much insurance you will need.

🔑 Insure the primary income resource.

Normally, the husband is the primary income resource and so his policy should be significantly higher than the wife's. But if the wife is the primary income resource, her policy should be higher than the husband's. First, insure the primary income resource and then if there are funds, insure the second spouse.

Amount of coverage is dependent upon current outstanding bills, spouse's income, number of small children in the home, funeral expenses and additional liabilities that would occur at the death of either spouse. There are a range of predictions from five to ten times the annual income as the base line policy amount. However, liabilities or lack of liabilities can offset these amounts. Using your life financial plan will assist you and your spouse in determining the correct amount of insurance you will need at this time in your life.

🔑 Insure the husband.

If the husband is the primary source of income and there are children in the home, a good minimum base coverage should start at $100,000 and will probably range somewhere between $300,000 and $500,000 depending upon liabilities. If the husband is not the primary source of income, then the base coverage should start at $25,000 and increase depending upon liabilities.

🔑 Insure the wife.

If the wife is the primary source of income, and there are children in the home. Use the husband's recommendations for insuring her. If the wife is not the primary income provider, you still need to insure her. I recommend securing an individual policy on the wife if you can afford a separate policy. Otherwise, include her as a rider on the husband's policy if possible. Note: If the wife is included on the husband's policy, she may lose her coverage upon the death of the husband and would have to acquire a new policy for herself at a higher premium. The policy could also be dependent upon insurability. The amount of insurance would be determined by the liabilities that would incur upon her death and how much income loss there would be if she worked. In determining the amount of coverage, consideration should be given for additional child care expense that the husband would incur if the wife died. Also, if her income offset other liabilities, the proration of her income against the husbands should be considered for the amount of coverage. In my opinion, unless the wife's income is significant in proportion to the husbands, a range of $25,000 to $50,000 coverage is adequate to cover the liabilities that would be incurred upon her death. Remember, life insurance is not to make the spouse rich.

🔑 Don't over insure children.

Often, I see parents that have bought life insurance policies of significant amounts for their children. I don't normally recommend individual policies for children, and I don't recommend large amounts of coverage. Children do not produce income resources to offset liabilities. Normally the only liability you will need to cover in the event of a child's death would be the burial expense. Today's average burial expense is about $7,500. This would be the maximum coverage you would need. If you are not able to meet this liability through your savings then I would recommend offsetting it with a small policy until you have prepared for this liability. Most primary policies for the parents will allow the children to be added as a rider on the primary policy at a much lesser expense than purchasing individual policies. A rider for $5,000 to $10,000 will cover burial expenses.

🔑 Avoid insuring other family members where possible.

The only reason you would insure any other family member would be against any liability you might incur upon their death. For example, you may have an elderly parent for whom you would be responsible for their burial expenses because they have not prepared for death costs, and you don't have the savings to cover that expense. In these situations, again you should only purchase enough insurance to offset the liability you can't meet. Sadly, in most situations you will be required to purchase a guaranteed life policy that has at least a two-year waiting period before it will pay the face value. However, some of these policies will at least reimburse your premium with some interest in the event of death prior to the waiting period so it does act like a savings account.

🔑 Avoid buying accidental insurance, indemnity plans, cancer policies, credit policies, or other specialty policies

sold by insurance companies, banks, credit card companies, and even retail companies.

When I was going through insurance school, we learned accidental policies are cheap because the insurance companies pay out less than 2 percent of all policies in force. I doubt those statistics have changed very much in the last twenty years.

I'm confident that the same payout is true with all the specialty policies. These type policies are great money makers for insurance companies. As an insurance agent, I would not sell any of these policies. I would rather sell you $1 of life insurance that would pay your beneficiary regardless of how you died than $10,000 of accidental insurance that only paid if you die in an accident. Likewise, my opinion applies to all the specialty policies. It just makes good common sense if you need liabilities protected and you are not self insured for you to invest in an insurance policy that will pay regardless of how you die.

🔑 Buy term life insurance versus whole-life-type policies.

I dealt with this subject of life insurance in chapter 5. However, I would like to expand some upon it. I spent eight years as an independent insurance agent. I went through the schools and learned what to say to close deals. I primarily sold adjustable life rather than the other type policies. I believed upon the training I received that it was the better deal. It had a lower premium than regular whole life policies and yet built cash surrender value. After I went through my financial crisis, I took a better look at insurance and came to the following conclusions:

Whole life policies, in my opinion, are simply overpriced! To accumulate cash surrender values, they must charge too much for the life insurance. The actual cash surrender value usually is less than the projected value. Any policy, whether it is called adjustable life, universal life, or whatever name used today that builds cash surrender value, is only a variation of a whole life policy.

Term insurance, in my opinion, is the best buy! Term policies are sold in various forms.

The annual renewable policy simply means the policy is good for one year and can be renewed the next year at the age appropriate rate. This type of policy is great if you need a lot of coverage for a short term.

In addition, many insurance companies offer fixed-level term five-, ten-, and twenty-year renewable policies. This simply means you can have a fixed premium for a specific period of time and then the rate increases. If there is a need to renew, you would simply renew at the age appropriate rate. I own and recommend the twenty-year-level term policy. Because I was not fully self-insured at the age of forty-five, I bought a policy at a very reasonable rate that will expire when I'm sixty-five. This gave me the ability to invest to become self-insured by age sixty-five.

These fixed level term policies are cheaper so you can buy adequate coverage at a reasonable rate rather than over priced whole life and the many variations of whole life insurance. These fixed level term policies will cover raising children liabilities, give you time to get out of debt, and give you time to prepare to be self-insured!

People often ask, "What about the surrender value of whole life policies? Is this not a good way to save money?" This is not the best way to invest, in my opinion, and many other financial counselors agree. Instead, find a good twenty-year term policy and take the difference in premium and invest it in a mutual fund or other investment.

This is what I did moving toward becoming self-insured. I invested first through my employer into a 403B mutual fund. At the age of fifty-nine, I pulled out of the market and rolled over the profit into an IRA to protect my retirement from market down turns. I can tell you a whole life policy would never have matched the market investment. Many insurance companies offer annuities; however, I believe you will do better with mutual funds or other investments than with annuities. I will talk more about retirement investments in chapter 7.

Reminder: Pay off your debts first with the savings before investing! Again, if for some reason you need large coverage for a short term, buy an annual renewable term policy.

Regardless of the life insurance policy, you choose, shop various companies to get the best deal. You can find some great deals on the internet, but check out the company's ratings, check with the Better Business Bureau, and check their licensing with your State Insurance Commission before purchasing. If they are not licensed in your state and you have a problem, you will have no options. Also, you can normally find cheaper policies at an independent insurance agent than with companies that only sell their policies. The independent agent has the ability to review the policies offered by the multiple companies they represent to get you the best coverage at the most reasonable rate. I would suggest allowing several independent agents to give you a quote as they may represent different insurance companies.

Remember this important key:

🔑 **Insurance is for liabilities you can't afford to self-insure.**

Buying large insurance policies just to profit off someone's death reveals a spiritual problem of not trusting God, and the spiritual problem of greed!

HEALTH INSURANCE POLICIES

There are a lot of health insurance plans on the market and premiums depend upon your age, your sex, your health history, and your social behavior. I will not go into details for all the available plans but will give you a brief overview. As always, I recommend you counsel with highly knowledge people that care about you prior to making major decisions.

I spoke some on this subject in chapter 5. Let's face it, health insurance is terribly expensive but major medical conditions like cancer and heart disease can financially bankrupt the average family. However, I do have some recommendations to keep your premiums as low as possible.

🔑 Self-insure yourself and your family as much as possible.

Don't try to cover every physician's expense and expenses for such things as well care, routine vaccinations, etc. Choose a policy that allows you to pay as much out of your pocket as possible. This will keep you premiums lower.

🔑 Purchase employers medical plans.

Employers usually are paying at least 25 percent of the premium cost so your premiums will be much lower than individual plans. These plans often include better dental and eye care than individual plans at a lower cost.

🔑 Choose a large deductible and higher co-pay comprehensive medical plan.

The higher the deductible and the larger the co-pay, the lower the premiums will be for these policies. A comprehensive medical plan covers both doctors' and hospital expenses.

🔑 Choose only a major medical plan to cover hospital expenses.

Major medical plans cover only hospital expenses. If you can't afford the comprehensive plans, at least cover the hospital expenses that will often bankrupt you. Again, choose higher deductibles and larger co pays to lower premiums.

🔑 **Participate in health savings accounts.**

Some companies offer a health savings account. You can put a pretax set amount of dollars in this savings account to pay medical bills, deductibles, and even for some over the counter medications and equipment your insurance doesn't cover. Warning: You need to estimate possible out of pockets expenses as closely to your history as possible. Any funds remaining in the account at the end of the accounting year is kept by most companies. Sit down with your company personnel representative to get a full understanding of how the company plan operates.

You can also start an independent health savings account at a bank or insurance company. Again, this plan requires a high deductible medical plan, and you will need to estimate your medical bills to determine required deposits. However, unlike employer plans, any unused funds in an independent medical savings accounts can be rolled over and used the next year or rolled into an IRA. Check with providers to see options available with their company.

INDEPENDENT SPECIALTY POLICIES: DENTAL, VISION, HEARING, DISABILITY, HOSPITAL INDEMNITY, CANCER, MEDICARE SUPPLEMENTAL POLICIES, AND LONG TERM CARE POLICIES

🔑 **Avoid most specialty policies.**

We have already spoken some on this issue in chapter 5. Insurance companies offer many variations of specialty plans. Disease policies, such as cancer policies, only pay if you contract the particular disease covered by the policy. Indemnity plans simply pay you a fixed amount for every day you are in the hospital. Medicare supplement policies cover the 20 percent that

Medicare requires you to pay. Warning: Medicare supplement polices generally will not pay medical expenses Medicare will not pay. Long-term care policies are designed to help cover the expensive cost of the need for extended care at home and assisted living facilities or nursing homes in event of a terminal illness or injury. These Long-term care plans can be useful in giving some protection to your life savings so as not to leave your spouse in a financial crisis. Although some websites report that over 40 percent of people receiving long-term care services are under the age of sixty-five, it has been recommended to me to wait until sixty years of age before purchasing a long-term care plan. I would advise consulting with an attorney specializing in estate planning, wills, etc. for your specific situation and alternative ways to protect your assets.

During the eight years, I was an insurance agent, I never sold these policies. I didn't believe these type independent policies were worth the premiums for the benefits provided. Independent dental, vision, hearing, and disability policies were more expensive than employer plans and offer far less benefits. I believed long-term I would be ahead, financially self-insuring myself instead of purchasing these independent policies. With the possible exception of long-term care plans, as of today I haven't seen anything that would change my mind. Since 1996 when I was laid off, I have had dental and eye care services and have been in the hospital several times with some lost wages. However, I believe the financial numbers have very much calculated in my favor by being self-insured rather than paying monthly insurance premiums. Understand that there are always exceptions, but the average person will most likely be ahead financially self-insuring themselves rather than paying premiums for these type of policies.

I believe it to be of greater benefit to purchase health insurance that will pay for any sickness, and invest the premiums for these specialty policies in a savings or money market account or other investments where the funds are easily accessible and drawing interest and then pay cash for the benefits these policies would provide.

ALTERNATIVE MEDICAL COVERAGE

🔑 **Join a Christian non-profit association medical sharing plan that assists with medical bills instead of investing into insurance companies.**

We have spoken some on this subject in chapter 5. If you have a heart to help people while providing for your own needs, in my opinion, a non-profit association plan is the plan for you. Warning: These sharing plans are not insurance. Otherwise, they would be subject to state insurance laws! However, at least two of the Christian non-profit associations sharing plans has been approved to exempt you from the presently enacted federal health care law.

These plans allow you to help fellow members instead of insurance executives. Your monthly dues pay the bills of fellow members directly. The dues for these plans are usually lower than insurance company's premiums even for high deductible plans. This is possible as these non-profit associations require that you have lived and continue to live healthy, Christian lifestyles to be a member. They also do not share medical bills with other members for pre-existing conditions although the Christian association I belong to will upon request include in their monthly dues notice non-sharing bills. This gives the membership the liberty to receive personal inspiration to give above their monthly due by sending a love offering directly to the individual with the non-shared expense. They also inform you of who your dues are being sent to assist and encourage cards and letters be sent to the person along with prayer. These plans do not guarantee payment of your medical bills as payment is dependent upon the members sending the contributions. However, Ann and I have been members of Christian Care Medi-Share since 2001, and every sharable bill has been paid.[2] Although there is a deductable per incident of sickness, I have found my out-of-pocket expenses have been far less than plans offered by insurance companies, plus I have the savings from the lower dues compared to higher insurance premiums. Therefore, I highly recommend Christian non-profit association plans in which the members are exempted from the federal insurance mandate. Search the internet and ensure the plan you choose will be exempt for members.

FEDERAL AND STATE SUBSIDIZED MEDICAL CLINICS

Another alternative to medical insurance is to use a clinic that is subsidized by either the federal or state government. Larger cities have these clinics to assist low income earners to receive low cost medical treatment and low cost prescriptions. The charges for services rendered are based upon household income. You will be required to provide proof of income and the birth certificates of each family member. Use the internet or the local telephone directory to locate facilities nearest you.

FREE CLINICS

In some cities, local charities and doctors will offer free medical clinics to the poor. Eligibility is based upon income. The types of procedures and test performed may be limited. Often, the operational days are limited to weekdays. Check with local charities or even the hospital to see if a free clinic operates in your city.

FREE AND REDUCED MEDICATIONS

Most major pharmaceutical companies offer a free medication program for individuals who cannot afford the monthly cost of medications. You can get free applications from the pharmaceutical company's website. Be aware: There are numerous websites offering to secure you free or reduced medications for a small application fee or for each drug ordered. If you have several prescriptions, you can use Partnership for Prescription Assistance.[3] It is one of several really free online websites that will qualify you and allow you to fill out applications online to take to your doctor.

There are also several companies that can be found on the internet that offer discount prescriptions. RX Outreach is one of several websites that offer discount drugs.[4] I usually buy six months of medications for the same price I would pay for forty-five days of medication at a local pharmacy. Only medications that have generics are available on these sites.

Eligibility for free and reduced medication is based upon income. These programs require your doctor's approval and a prescription. These plans must be renewed annually.

I have used several pharmaceutical programs for free medication in the past when my income was very low and found them to be excellent. You will need to get your physician to write two prescriptions. One to be filled immediately by a local pharmacy as it takes about three to four weeks to get approved by the pharmaceutical company and receive your first prescription in the mail. The second prescription will normally be for one year unless the drug is a narcotic in which case the drug company will have additional requirements to met government guidelines. Most drugs will be mailed directly to your home, but some will be required to be sent directly to your doctor.

INDIGENT CARE

This is probably one of the most abused programs available at hospitals. The heart of these programs was to help the poor to obtain emergency medical treatment and to give the hospital some reimbursement for expenses. Sadly, you can go into any hospital and find the waiting lobby full of individuals with minor sicknesses creating backlogs for the medical staff. Usually, the city or county is subsidizing this care. Poverty level income is the requirement, and you must ask hospital staff for assistance to get this care.

CHARITABLE CARE

Some charitable organizations attach themselves to hospitals and offer financial assistance to the poor and needy. Again, income determines the availability of assistance. Ask the hospital staff if any charitable organizations are available for your medical situation. You can also find organizations on the internet that assist with major diseases like cancer.

MEDICARE

🔑 **Register for Medicare three months prior to reaching age sixty-five.**

Most people are not aware they need to register for Medicare three months prior to reaching age sixty-five to avoid possible penalties. Even if you are not planning on retiring at age sixty-five, you will need to register for Medicare. Since the eligible full retirement age for many people has changed to sixty-six or sixty-seven, I fear many individuals will be caught in the penalty dilemma. Therefore, three months prior to reaching age sixty-five, go to your local Social Security office or you can register online to ensure you avoid any penalties.

Medicare is a federal plan. When signing up for Medicare you can choose the basic plans of part A, B, and D, or you can choose an insurance company to administer your health benefits. Some of these insurance plans can cover items and medical procedures that Medicare does not. I personally like the insurance expanded coverage over the basic Medicare plans. There are a lot of plans available so research them thoroughly to ensure you are getting what you need and can afford.

MEDICAID

🔑 **Inquire at the Social Security office to see if you qualify.**

This is a state plan. Individuals at poverty and below poverty income can qualify for this medical coverage. Since these plans are administered by the state, the requirements and coverage will vary from state to state. Usually there are no deductibles and medications are free with theses plans. Ask the representative at the Social Security office in your city how to apply.

STORE MERCHANDISE EXTENDED WARRANTY PROTECTION PLANS

🔑 **Avoid these plans and save your money.**

I don't recommend buying merchandise protections plans. In my opinion, they are overpriced for the benefit and seldom are redeemed. They are a real money maker for retail stores. Most merchandise you buy such as appliances and electronics comes with at least a one-year manufacturer's warranty. Some retail stores also give you a thirty- to ninety-day return policy if the item breaks. Normally, defects will appear within the first ninety days or long after those extended warranty policies. So in most situations, between the store warranty and the manufacturer's warranty, you will be covered. I believe you will be better off to put the warranty money in a savings account and draw interest. In the event you did have a failure of the equipment, you would have this money to help offset the expense, and if there was no failure, you have just made yourself additional money to spend on something you desire.

BUYING A HOME

🔑 **Buy only according to your needs and what you can afford.**

Everyone probably would desire that home on the ocean front that is a mansion. For most of us, this is not reasonable. Still, most families buy more home than they can afford and/or really need! Looking at the homes of the average family in the early history of our country, we see small, one-room log cabins that housed families of eight to ten people. Even most post–World War II homes were modest homes of 1,000 square feet or less. Most of my childhood homes were very simple with one-to-two bedrooms. Often all the children slept in one bedroom and the parents slept in another. Now, parents think each child must have their own bedroom. Also, there must be at least two bathrooms and in some homes, a bathroom for almost every bedroom. There is nothing wrong with this as long as you can afford it and are faithful to fully follow God's plans as outlined in scripture for disbursement of wealth.

Determining how large of a home to purchase is dependent upon your actual needs, your income, and other expenses. As discussed in previous chapters, in no situation should the income of both spouses be considered when determining the home you can afford. Normally, you will use the husband's income to make that determination. As I have previously explained, sickness can affect any spouse and can have a dramatic impact on your financial situation. But wives usually bear children and the loss of their income for even a short period of time can create a crisis on your financial situation if your basic living needs require their support. This may put you in jeopardy of losing your home; therefore, always use the husband's income to determine what you can afford to buy. Be sure to take into account utilities, taxes, insurance, and maintenance as part of your total purchasing power. If the wife chooses to work, let her income buy the furnishings.

🔑 Best home buys are repossessions and short-sale homes.

At the writing of this book, the recession has put a lot of surplus homes on the market. Many people lost their jobs and were required to take positions paying less. Many families were struggling prior to losing their jobs to make the monthly mortgage payments and, thus, banks foreclosed when they could not make the payments. Now, many banks are selling off some of the properties they have held for an extended time far below their investment. You can find these homes on the internet and contract a real estate agent to bid on bank short sale homes for you.

Most people don't have the cash money to purchase a home, and so I recommend your initial home cost should never exceed three and one half times the husband's net income. A gross income of $40,000 paying a combined total of 20 percent federal and state taxes after adjustments would net $32,000 qualifying for a $112,000 home. The monthly mortgage payment at 5 percent interest for thirty years would be $601.24 or about 24 percent of the net annual income. When you add the utilities, taxes, insurance, and maintenance cost to the mortgage, the total cost percentage should not exceed 35 percent of net income. From these numbers, you can see why I say most people buy more house than they can afford putting themselves and their family in financial jeopardy.

Owning your own home is probably the most expensive personal expenditure you will ever make. Most people just don't have enough savings to be able to pay cash money so the option is to take out a mortgage. If you find yourself in a position requiring a mortgage, then you may find the following tips useful:

🔑 Secure a thirty-year mortgage and discipline yourself to make fifteen-year payments.

Some financial advisors recommend you select a fifteen-year mortgage instead of a thirty-year mortgage. However, I believe the better option would be to secure a thirty-year mortgage and make the fifteen-year monthly payment. I believe this is a safer option than securing a thirty even if you pay a little more interest. My reasoning is if you are laid off from work or have a brief sickness where cash flow is decreased, it will be easier during that period to temporarily reduce your payment to the fifteen-year payment thus possibly avoiding a foreclosure. If you set up a fifteen-year mortgage, you have no way to temporarily reduce your payments, and this could put you in a position of default and repossession. Having the ability to reduce your payments could get you through a temporary crisis and save your home. You should return back to making the fifteen-year payment amounts as quickly as possible.

- **Add additional money to your monthly mortgage payment as you get extra money to spend.**

Remember, the goal is to get out of debt. Adding only five dollars a month to your mortgage payment can reduce months off your loan period and thousands of dollars in interest.

- **Make sure you notify the mortgage company that any money you prepay each month is for principle only.**

Otherwise, they may apply any additional payments toward monthly payments pushing out the due date for the next payment and not reducing interest.

- **Write two checks!**

Write one check for principle only, and the other for the monthly mortgage payment! This would be true for any loan where you make additional payments. Your goal is to become debt-free so ever dime increase will make this dream a reality much sooner.

🔑 **Split your monthly mortgage payment in half and make a payment every two weeks.**

This also will reduce the amount of interest you pay. By making a payment every other week, you will make an extra month's payment every year. Contact your lender to see if this is allowed.

RENTAL DWELLINGS

Every person I know wants their own home, but the reality is that everyone cannot afford to own a home. I see nothing in Scripture that guarantees every person will own a home. Some people just can't get a loan. Rental dwellings are their only option unless they move back in with their parents. In some situations, temporarily moving back into the parent's homes may be the best option to save money until you are financially prepared to get into a place of your own. I do caution that if you move back into your parent's home, you remember it is their home and even though you are an adult; you abide by their rules with respect. Also, generously share in the expenses of utilities, rent or mortgage costs, household supplies and food, and assist in general housekeeping and yard maintenance. Remember your parents are doing you a favor. Don't take advantage of their generosity. Give them more than they ask of you with a good spirit. You are not there to add an additional burden on them. They are already burdened knowing your financial distress as they desire the best for you. Use the following keys for securing and maintaining rental dwellings.

🔑 **Compare rental prices for like dwellings and consider the age of dwellings.**

You could be getting a low monthly rental rate, but it could be poorly insulated driving the utilities cost much higher than a new dwelling renting at a higher price. I have seen houses that rent for $400 to $500 dollars a month with $300 and $400 utility bills. Most new apartment's utilities will run between $90 and $135 a month. They could be the better deal even though the rental price is higher.

🔑 **Take extensive photos of each room of the rental property prior to moving in and then again when you move out to guard your deposits.**

🔑 **Choose a smaller unit than you desire to reduce the rental cost and save the difference for a deposit on your own home.**

Rent a two bedroom and put bunk beds in one room for the kids. They *will* survive! Read your history books or even ask your grandparents about their childhood. This will also give you and your family the incentive to work together to accomplish your goals.

BUYING CLOTHES

🔑 **Name brand doesn't always mean better quality.**

When I was working in a discount retail store, I noticed the vendor was going to other major retail stores within the mall. Upon questioning him I discovered he was selling each store the same shirt the discount retailer was selling only under a different name for each major retail chain store. I have an aunt who worked for a shirt manufacturer several years ago. She says they would make the shirts, box them and store them until a buyer placed an order. Once the order was placed, they removed the boxes of shirts and sewed in the label for that particular retailer. Again the same shirt, but the label depended upon the purchaser. I'm confident this is practiced not only by the shirt manufacturers, but also for many other clothing items. It makes economical sense that a manufacturer would make their product available to a vast market rather than only a select retail chain. Often, discount retailers must remove labels of name brand items before they are allowed to sell items to comply with major retailers' requirements to the manufacturer's overstocked items.

Ann is one of the best when it comes to getting the best bargains on clothes. She not only shops the discount retailers, but some of the major retail chain stores. Normally, Ann will buy clothes at less than twenty-five percent of the retail price. I'm usually not the clothing buyer in my home. Therefore, I have asked Ann to share some of her buying keys to help you get the best bargains so you too can take advantage of her buying wisdom.

🔑 Wait until stores offer an additional 40 percent off already marked down sales tags to shop.

Stores like JCPenney, Belk, and Sears will put their seasonal items on sale twice a year around February to March and again from July to August. Look for the red, yellow, and green sale stickers and take the additional 40 percent off the marked down price. Ann does her major shopping during these sales and gets her best bargains. She has bought name-brand tops for $3, name-brand shoes for $8 or less, and name-brand purses for $6.

🔑 Look for clearance items in the aisle displays.

Often, retailers desiring to move items fast will display the clearance items on counters or end racks to grab your attention. Ann finds great bargains not only on clothes but toys, crafts, and many other household goods on these displays.

🔑 Look for the clearance racks among the clothing racks.

Clothing retailers will place clearance items so you will have to walk pass the regular priced items in hopes of enticing you to pick up other items as well as the clearance items. Ann doesn't care if the clothes are not name brand as long as the price is right. The one exception is that Ann likes Gloria Vanderbilt jeans. However, she never buys Gloria Vanderbilt jeans unless they are on sale.

🗝 Use store coupons to save additional off the marked down prices.

One example of Ann's great savings was when a store was offering Gloria Vanderbilt jeans on sale for $19.99. Ann applied the $10 off store coupon and bought the jeans for $9.99 plus sales tax. She says, "What a price to pay for a pair of Gloria Vanderbilt jeans!"

Seldom does she need to purchase additional clothing beyond these special additional 40 percent off already marked down price sales events.

🗝 Utilize the special sales for Christmas, birthdays, weddings, and baby showers gifts.

Ann is not only able to purchase for herself and me, but for our children and grandchildren for birthdays and Christmas along with gifts for weddings and baby showers for our friends and family at great savings. Ann just stores the items until the occasion occurs.

🗝 A bargain is not a bargain if you can't afford it or don't need it.

Ann has always been a great shopper, and early in our marriage, she bought far too many items. She believed the items were bargains because they were on sale. However, after our financial crisis, she practices that a bargain is not a bargain if you can't afford it or don't need it.

BUYING FOOD

Review chapter 5 for additional subject matter. As with clothing, I'm not the food buyer for our family. Again, I'm leaning upon Ann's expertise to share keys to get the best bargains.

🔑 **Name brand items are not always better.**

Ann says some store brand-items taste better than some name brand items and are cheaper. Let your family test them without knowing they are not name brands. Don't tell them it is not name brand and don't ask them if they like it. They will let you know if they don't like the item.

🔑 **Review the sales papers and plan your meals accordingly.**

Ann looks on the internet to find bargains as well as publications we receive in the mail and in the local newspapers. Not only does she save at the grocery stores, but she clips the coupons for eating out at restaurants and fast food chains. She really likes buying one and getting the second of equal or lesser value free—and so do I.

🔑 **Compare grocery stores prices.**

Make out a normal grocery list and research the stores to see which store offers the best savings on the items you normally buy.

🔑 **Use coupons.**

Use internet, newspaper, and magazine coupons where they give you the better bargain. Attend coupon classes to learn how to be a good coupon shopper. Research the internet for available coupon classes in your area. Some churches and financial institutions offer classes.

Although store and manufacturer coupons are great, Ann doesn't use many because often the store brand item is cheaper than the name brand even with a coupon. Ann and I know some people are partial to name brands; therefore, we often lay the unused coupons on the shelf in front of the item for another shopper to use. Review chapter 5 recommendations for how to best use manufacturers' coupons.

🔑 Research for the best days to get real bargains from a food retailer.

Often, stores will have a set day each week when they mark down meat and other items. Some stores offer double and even triple coupon value days. It's often worth the effort to shop on those days.

🔑 Increment your shopping.

Buy and store reasonable amounts of sale items where you buy one and get one free. This week, you might focus on meats; next week, can goods; next week, packaged goods; and the next week, household items. Ann purchases meats on sale, and if it's not needed for that week, she will put the extra pieces in the freezer. Larger packages of meats are usually cheaper and can be individually wrapped and stored in the freezer for future use.

I'm sure Ann has many other keys for buying bargains and saving that I have missed. However, just applying the keys she has shared will save you a lot of money.

BUYING APPLIANCES AND ELECTRONIC DEVICES

🔑 **Buy with cash where possible.**

Become a *negotiator*! Research the internet and get the best price you can find on the item. Then offer the retailer less than that in cash. Cash talks! If the retailer will not accept your offer, you can always go to another retailer and do the same. Be patient and persistent! If the retailer can make money, and especially if business is slow, there is a good chance they will sell you the product for a lower cost.

🔑 **Request price matching.**

If you can't buy it for less, then take the printout of the price you found and ask the retailer if they have a matching price program. Most major appliance stores will do a price match. I saved a family member $247 on a $700 appliance by using this plan. I saved myself an additional $200 on a washing machine that was reduced by $100 by simply showing the printout of an internet advertisement. Receive even more of a bargain by using your credit card that gives you rewards or cash back. But only use a credit card if you have developed the habit of paying the full balance monthly.

🔑 **Buy simple!**

My dad taught me the more features something has; the more it cost, and the more it cost to repair. Most likely, you will never use all those features anyway so save the money!

🔑 **Forget the extended warranties.**

I remind you to put the money you would use to pay for extended warranties in a savings account and let it be your warranty. You can then use it if you need a repair! Most likely, it will still be in the bank long after the extended warranty expires. Extended warranties are great money makers for the companies, and they train and press their sales people to sell them.

INTERNET PURCHASES

The internet can be a great way to find bargains, and at the same time, you can easily be scammed. Following these keys will help avoid as much risk as possible:

🗝 **Check out the company before purchasing.**

There are a lot of scammers on the internet. There is safety in contacting the better business bureau of the city of the company's headquarters. You can also look for internet complaints against the company.

🗝 **Track credit card purchases.**

Immediately follow up with your credit card company to make sure there is only one charge when you have made a purchase, and make sure it is correct. Do this for, at least, three months to ensure there are no additional charges. File a fraud complaint with your credit card company if there are additional charges or if you didn't receive the merchandise.

🗝 **Use PayPal accounts.**

Using bank account drafts are an unwise option unless the company is local and well established. I would advise a separate checking account with minimum funds to cover PayPal purchases rather than linking to your primary account. If there is a breach in security, your loss will be minimal, and you can easily close the account without major changes to established payment drafts.

- **Avoid internet companies that advertise their products that give you a thirty-day money back guarantee with automatic shipments.**

I learned this lesson the hard way. It is a nightmare to get refunds and to get them to stop shipping and charging you. You are probably talking to an agent in another country and will get a different agent every time you call. They will tell you they have put the stop shipment in the computer, but that is not always accurate. Do the research to make sure the company is located in your home country when buying products online. Otherwise, eat your loss because it will be difficult to get your money back, and you may never get the merchandise.

CREDIT CARD PAYMENTS

- **Make credit card payments at least seven days before the due date.**

In speaking with associates at some credit card companies, I was informed that, sometimes, a payment can be classified as late even though it was postmarked and even made it to the mail room of the company on the due date. However, it did not make it to the accounting desk in time so it is considered late. The credit card representative told me payments are not considered late if the postmark is seven days prior to the due date.

- **Negotiate credit card rates.**

Your credit card company desires to keep you as a customer. Contact your credit card company if you receive a lower interest card offer. Most likely they will match the offer.

In closing this chapter, we could not possibly address every item available on the market, but we have given you examples of how to wisely purchase some primary items that are common to most every household.

Applying the keys we have shown you will assist you in becoming good stewards of God's wealth. He has entrusted you as his steward and your family will be blessed for doing so! They will assist you in getting that debt monkey off your back and living a life of being debt-free!

Pray this prayer in closing this chapter,

> Father, I thank you for all the knowledge and wisdom that you give me. Bring to my remembrance this knowledge and wisdom when I make purchases. Strengthen me to avoid temptations to violate the knowledge and wisdom in order that you might call me your wise servant and my family will be blessed. In Jesus's name, I ask! Amen.

PLANNING WISDOM

Every parent desires for their children to be happy and successful in life. Sadly, most parents fail to see the big picture and fail to plan. Often, this creates unnecessary hardships for the children when they become adults. Proper planning will give you a sense of peace and assist in helping your children to start out their adult life standing on their feet rather than trying to get up out of the mud. We will address some expenses that may seem very distant, but time will rapidly pass and catch you unprepared unless you start planning today.

CHILDREN'S EDUCATION

Most people wait until it is time for the children to go to college to figure out how they are going to pay for it. Grants and student loans are then utilized, or sometimes it's decided a child cannot go to college because they can't afford the expenses that will be incurred. Grants are tax-free money a child may receive if they meet the requirement qualifications, but student's loans must be paid back. We are not going to get into the details of either of these as the college counselors will provide information on their availability and how to apply for them. However, the problem with student loans I have encountered is that many graduates owe so much money in college loans it jeopardizes their financial situation after they graduate. Young couples looking to purchase a home and even to meet their basic living expenses find it very difficult to manage with the burden of student loan debts. Adding a child to the family can really put their financial situation in a crisis. I'm not persuaded that student loans are a good thing. As a parent, how can you help your children get the education they need without you or them falling into the trap of debt?

🔑 **Develop a plan for education cost beginning the day of a child's birth.**

Do you really desire for your children to start out their adult life with a debt monkey on their back? There are insurance annuity plans and state plans which provide tax-free revenues provided that your child goes to college. You can talk to your insurance agent or financial advisor concerning the available plans in your state. From the time a child is born until they are eighteen years of age, you have 936 weeks to save for education cost. Estimating a cost of $50,000 for education would require you to save approximately $53 a week for each child to keep them from being burdened with debt. If God has blessed you financially, the tax codes allow you to give your children up to $10,000 tax-free each year as advancement on their inheritance. This could be deposited into a joint savings account for your child and you. I would suggest you get with a lawyer to better understand your options and to determine what restrictions you could place on the savings or investment for withdrawals. Hopefully, by the time your child has reached age eighteen, you will have instilled many of the principles taught in this book to them, and they will have shown themselves to be good stewards.

If it was determined your child would attend a trade school which is often less expensive than college or decided to get a job instead of attending school, the money saved could be used to help them get started in a home.

CHILDREN'S MARRIAGE

We have already talked about this in previous chapters; more than likely, your child is going to get married. Yet many parents scramble to find the finances to pay for their children's wedding because they did not properly prepare themselves for this event. Sometimes parents even go into debt for the big event when this could easily be avoided with proper planning.

🔑 **Develop a special savings to pay for wedding ceremonies.**

Using the 936 weeks time frame would require saving approximately $5 a week to accumulate approximately $5,000 for a wedding. Even though this is a special day, most parents spend far too much money for the wedding leaving very little funds to assist their children in starting out their married life. Something seems to be broke in our thinking. Many parents jokingly have stated, "If only they would elope, I could give them this money to start out life." Aside from encouraging your children to elope, there is a way to help them and yourself financially.

🔑 **Keep the wedding ceremony simple.**

Do as much of the preparation for the wedding as you can. My wife's mother made my wife's beautiful wedding gown. My mother-in-law, along with my wife, some friends, and me fixed all the food. The beautiful cake was prepared by a friend of the family. We also decorated the church. It was a beautiful ceremony that we will never forget, but it didn't cost her parents a great sum of money. Keeping the cost down would provide the opportunity to financially assist the newly married couple in starting out life together.

CHILDREN'S FUTURE HOME

A home normally is the biggest expense your children will have in starting out life. They must acquire money for the down payment, insurance, and property taxes. Once they have secured the home, there is the furniture, curtains, appliances, pots, pans, dishes, cleaning supplies, and lawn care equipment. Even if they rent, still along with the deposit they will have most of the expenses of owning a home. All these expense are beyond must young couples means, so they get heavily in debt from the very beginning, and many struggle for the rest of their lives to survive.

It is like trying to swim with a block tied to your leg. You are stroking as hard as you can just to keep your nose above the water to survive.

Parents, you may know just what I'm talking about, because like me you have or are currently experiencing the same struggle. I know you love your children. I pray that what you have read so far in the book has stirred your spirit to the point that getting out of debt is not an option; it is must for your welfare and for the future of your children. Your children do not have to suffer as you have suffered.

This is the day to begin planning toward your children's future home. This is not something you can procrastinate on. I believe our culture in America has done a great injustice to the future generations. Seemly we have thrown our kids out into the ocean and told them to swim without a boat, without a paddle, without a life preserver, or any real provisions to survive. I don't believe we think of it that way, and yes, we do love our children. But we are passing on to them the only thing we know about survival, and it is insufficient.

God has a better plan, and it's time that we return to God's Word and see a culture that knew how to prepare their children for marriage, how to insure they had a home, and provisions to start out in life and to sustain them throughout their life through an early inheritance. You can read more under inheritance about how to use an inheritance to stop this destructive cycle of debt with proper planning.

I believe that the Old Testament and the New Testament gives some light in planning for our children's adult home. We will address this under the subject of inheritance.

EDUCATE YOUR CHILDREN ABOUT FINANCIAL MATTERS

🗝 **Start teaching your children at a young age about managing money.**

Let's face it, we can't depend upon the public or private schools to train our children in financial matters. The burden is upon us as parents. It is amazing how so many adults don't know how to keep a check registrar much less know how to balance the check registrar with a bank statement. Children need to be taught this and taught how to budget money. They need to know what records need to be kept for tax reporting. They need to know how and when to give! See the addendum for a sample budget for small children.

🗝 **Involve your children in your household finances.**

I tell all parents I counsel who are in a financial crisis to sit down regularly with their children who are at least ten years of age and open their bank statements and budgets for them to see. You will find that children understand more than we think. If they see you are honest with them and did a good job explaining that even though there are X amount of dollars in the bank, they are committed to paying not only the weekly bills but insurance and/or repair bills that will be coming due in six months, they will understand. Most likely, they will ask for fewer things at that point because they understand you really can't afford to buy them. You should start training children younger than ten to budget. Don't always give them money but allow them to earn money and teach them to manage it with a simple budget. This budget should not allow them to spend all the money; it should allow a percent for immediate personal use, a percent for savings, and a percent for giving. The same is true for teens.

🔑 Teens should contribute toward expenses.

This is especially true if you are in a financial crisis and they are old enough to work. Let them work during the weekends and during the summer months and help with expenses. After all, they need to eat, have a roof over their heads, and have clothes and medical attention, so it is right that they contribute where it is needed. Allow them to keep a portion of their income for pocket money, a portion for giving, and the balance for assisting with household expenses. If you are financially stable then require them to put the household expense portion into a savings account for a future vehicle, college, marriage, etc. I have included a simple budget for small children in the addendum as well as one for teenagers. If you start from an early age instilling the principles of budgeting, they will be far ahead of most young adults in developing disciplined habits in managing financial matters.

INHERITANCE

Tradition in America is to leave an inheritance to our children to be dispersed at our death. The parent's heart is pure to bless their children by leaving an inheritance. However, inheritances often become a curse to a family. I say this because I have seen many situations where inheritances caused divisions among even close siblings no matter how small the amount of the inheritance and no matter the age of the siblings. The inheritance may not even be needed by the siblings, but if there is an inheritance, sometimes the real heart of a person (which is often greedy) will be revealed, and they will fight over the inheritance even if it is small. I've also seen where children gave up their rightful inheritance—their humility—to prevent trouble with their siblings. I'm sure no parent would be happy to know their children were fighting over an inheritance. There must be a better way to bless our children and to prevent division.

🔑 Give the bulk of an inheritance to your children at critical periods in their lives.

Let me say that long ago, I determined my parents owed me nothing. As far as I'm concerned, I have already received my inheritance from both my parents. They suffered and sacrificed to provide the best they could for me during my childhood and have blessed me in various ways during their lifetime.

I believe there is a better way to give children an inheritance and a better time than them receiving it after your death! Why not give the bulk of financial inheritances at critical periods in your children's lives? College, marriage, and securing a home are examples of the critical periods in your children's lives and would be beneficial times to distribute an inheritance. I really can't determine when the practice of waiting until after death to give an inheritance began, but in the Old and New Testaments, I believe it seems to appear that at least a partial inheritance was given prior to the death of the parents. We see in Genesis 25 where Jacob receives a birthright, and in chapter 27, a blessing from his father Isaac. The Jewish custom was the espousal contract and then the son would return to his father's house, and they would prepare for receiving the bride. It seems the parents were involved through an inheritance in getting the couple in a home and off to a good financial start in life. In the New Testament, Jesus uses an illustration of a father giving an inheritance prior to death to illustrate a truth.

> And he said, A certain man had two sons:
> And the younger of them said to his father, Father, give me the portion of goods that falleth to me. And he divided unto them his living.
>
> Luke 15:11–12 (KJV)

Giving your children at least a partial inheritance while you are alive can give you great joy as you see how the inheritance blesses their lives. By giving them a financial inheritance upon reaching adulthood, you could possibly prevent them from a financial crisis! You could even give personal items to each child before you die. My mother has done this with each of her children, giving pictures, china, etc. By giving the items now, she has the joy of seeing the smiles on her children's faces and seeing them enjoying the gifts. There are a few items still in her house that will be distributed according to her wishes upon her death. You don't have to give your children all their inheritance now! At death, your will could direct your estate be sold giving each child or grandchild a small, equal, monetary amount with the remaining balance being given to your church or a charitable organization to help others. I have heard of some parents who bought insurance policies equal to the value of their estate with their children as equal beneficiaries. They then willed their entire estate to a church or charitable institution. This way, they were confident their children would not be fighting over items.

After what I have seen over my lifetime, I personally believe it to be better to give the bulk inheritances to your children and grandchildren while you are alive. Designate in your will to sell and distribute the remaining amounts equally among your family, church, or charity of choice. Rather than giving a lump sum of cash, I would suggest bestowing a small amount of spending cash to each of your children with any greater sums to be put in the children's retirement accounts or toward paying off a mortgage if they are struggling financially. Bless young grandchildren by bestowing an amount in a savings account toward educational funds, car, or a future home. If the grandchildren are married, bestow an amount toward paying a lump sum on their mortgage or toward a retirement fund. Talk with your lawyer about your best options to disperse your estate at death.

PLAN FOR RETIREMENT

Unless you die or the rapture takes place, there will come a time in your life when you may not be able to perform the functions of your job due to illness requiring you to retire early or because of age you decide to retire from the workforce. Planning now for retirement is prudent. People look for a long life and forward to a day when they can retire from the work force. They are always hoping for a time when they can enjoy whatever pleasure they desire without the restrictions of having to ask their boss for time off or deal with financial restrictions. Prior to the Social Security Act, people worked until they physically or mentally could not work, or until they had saved enough money to sustain a particular lifestyle. The Bible is almost silent on the issue of retirement. There is only one reference in the Old Testament concerning the duties of a Levite.

> And from the age of fifty years they shall cease waiting upon the service thereof, and shall serve no more: But shall minister with their brethren in the tabernacle of the congregation, to keep the charge, and shall do no service. Thus shalt thou do unto the Levites touching their charge.
>
> Numbers 8:25–26 (KJV)

In these two verses, retirement still isn't explained as we know of it today.

🔑 Retirement in the Bible is a change of occupation.

At age fifty, the Levite was no longer doing the physical labor of carrying the tent, ceremonial utensils, and preparing and cleaning everything associated with the sacrifices. Their role changed from a physical to more of a supervisory and teaching role overseeing the training of the younger Levites and ensuring everything was done properly in a reverent manner according to the instructions God had given unto Moses. God was giving honor to these older Levites whom were past their prime for the physical labors involved in servicing the people of God and using their maturity and knowledge to train and keep reverent order of administration in the house of God.

When we look at retirement as a change of occupation, we see many opportunities to be able to minister in capacities that were not possible while employed in the secular work force. Many small churches with limited financial resources are in need of volunteer staffing to expand their ministry capabilities. Perhaps, God has ordained you good health and financial resources at retirement to participate in kingdom work.

Since the Bible is silent on retirement as we know it today, when an individual stops working, we cannot condemn this practice. This then puts us back into a situation of planning for the day we can permanently leave the workforce. This requires laying aside the proper amount of funds to sustain a particular lifestyle. Social Security for many years has been a method of assisting us to move toward this goal. However, it was never intended to be the sole method of preparing for retirement. As I told you, my father worked as a mechanic until he had a stroke at the age of seventy. Likewise, my mother worked a physical job in a factory until she was forced at the age of seventy to retire because she was not physically able to perform the job they was going to require her to do after she suffered from a stroke. Neither my father nor mother had put money aside for retirement. Because of their failure to save, their living standards were greatly diminished after retirement. I believe both would have worked until they dropped dead on the job if they had been given a choice rather than retiring to such a drastic change in lifestyle.

In my counseling duties, I find many seniors are in a financial crisis because of a lack of planning and depending solely upon Social Security to meet their needs. The reality is Social Security can't adequately provide the basic necessities for many. Either they must return to the workforce performing very low paying jobs or depend upon financial assistance from family and their church. Is this really the lifestyle you desire? If not, then it is important for you to do as follows:

🗝 **Immediately begin a savings and investment program to prepare for retirement.**

The very tool of Social Security many seniors of my day have depended upon will basically expire for future generations. For many years, there has been a gradual reduction in the monthly checks to seniors not keeping up with inflation. With the threat of going bankrupt, congress is looking for ways to drastically reduce the payout of Social Security benefits and to even phase it out. It is of immense priority for future generations to plan to replace Social Security with personal savings if you ever desire to retire with dignity.

In the previous chapters, we spoke much about developing a frugal lifestyle today in order to save for tomorrow. I can't stress enough that if you don't develop this habit of saving right now, you will find yourself in a financial crisis at retirement. We have also given you a simple plan to begin saving.

🗝 **Invest most of your raises from this day forward into a 401k or an IRA account.**

Most companies today still offer an investment match up to 6 percent of your income. This is a great bargain so be sure to take advantage of it if it is available. I don't know where you can easily get this kind of return upfront. This will mean you will be required to keep your standard of living basically frugal unless you make a lot of money. Only accept a pay increase in your take home pay occasionally to offset inflation. Most companies give you the opportunity to invest your 401k investment to purchase company stock, mutual funds, or a fixed money market account. I personally like the mutual funds for 401k and IRA plans.

🔑 Rollover any company pension or 401K savings into a retirement account outside the company.

Many companies' pension funds are underfunded. This creates the potential you could lose your pension if the company declared bankruptcy. Therefore, I recommend when leaving your present employer for retirement or to take employment with another company, you roll over any pension and retirement funds into an IRA or possibly your new employers' 401k plan. Another option you may consider the following:

🔑 Create a 401k LLC or IRA LLC as an alternative investment plan for retirement.

I only recently learned about either of these plans as an alternative way to invest for your retirement. If you own a company, you can start the 401k LLC otherwise use the IRA LLC. These plans allow you to self direct the investment of your retirement dollars. The biggest plus to these plans is you can invest in most anything within the tax code guidelines. The biggest obstacle is finding a lawyer and a CPA that is knowledgeable in this area to set them up with check writing privileges on the account. The IRA LLC plan requires a custodian to manage the fund. In a truly self-directed 401K LLC or IRA LLC account, I'm told you can be that custodian! Check with your lawyer! However, there are several companies that will allow you to open these accounts with their company as long as they are the custodians. Most that I have found charge high fees for each transaction of deposit. You will need the assistance of a knowledgeable lawyer and CPA if you desire to set up a totally self-directed account. Otherwise, you can use the companies that assume the custodial role and can establish the plan for you. Although, nearly all my retirement has previously been invested in mutual funds, I pulled out of the stock market in recent months due to the uncertainty of the market. Twice, I had lost a major portion of my investment. Historically, you can recover within ten years. But I am sixty, and I can't afford this great loss again if I'm to retire in a few short years. Therefore, I have decided a self-directed **IRA LLC** or **401k LLC** is my best option over the unstable stock market. I'm working with a lawyer and CPA at the writing of this book to set this up for me.

🔑 **Regardless of what plan you use for retirement, start saving and investing today for tomorrow!**

Saving and investing is extremely important if you ever hope to retire. In previous chapters, we taught you the following key:

🔑 **Failing to plan and take action is planning to fail!**

Start today to develop a plan and put it into action, so you may reap the rewards of proper planning and faithfulness in your *older* days.

PLAN FOR DEATH

We have already spoken some on this issue in chapter 6. But because most of us would like to put it out of our minds, thinking if won't happen to us, I want to stress again there are two certain things in life. You were born, and you are going to die unless Jesus comes before your death happens. Most people procrastinate when dealing with details about death, leaving their grieving loved ones with the burden of funeral and burial arrangements and often the associated financial cost. Is this really fair to them? I don't think so! Proper planning will soften the burden for those that love you the most.

🔑 **Develop a written informational package.**

Sit down and prepare a written informational package for your loved ones to use in the event of your death. Include all necessary documents with this package, and store it in a secure place such as a fire proof safe or bank vault. If you store it in a bank vault, make sure your spouse and/or one other family member is named to have access to the vault. Make sure your immediate family knows about this package and where to find it. This package should include the following:

Financial Information such as checking, savings, investments, cash, mortgage loans, credit cards, life insurance premiums, health insurance premiums, cell phones, internet, satellite services, and/or any other debts. Also include the following:

🔑 Life Insurance and Health Insurance Policies

Be sure to include account numbers, addresses, contact names, phone numbers, and approximate balances as of a specific date. Leave instructions of where to find any cash money! Although I don't recommend it, some people like to hide money in walls, behind pictures, and between pages of books.

Burial information such as cemetery plots, vaults, markers, and funeral arrangements.

Sit down and talk with at least your spouse and possibly your minister to outline the type funeral service you desire, and put it in writing. If you desire to be cremated, this should be in the instructions. This will take a lot of pressure off your surviving family. Do it now! Don't procrastinate because you believe you have a long life in front of you. Young people die every day! I would suggest one of the first tasks you do in planning for your future is to prepare for your death.

🔑 Living will

Your family needs direction in the event of a catastrophic illness or injury. Do they put you on life support or not and under what conditions? A living will answers these questions. However, understand that if you go to the hospital, they will immediately need a copy of your living will in order to grant your wishes. I would suggest you talk with your attorney to get the best information concerning living wills and how to use them.

🔑 Durable power of attorney

At some point in your life, you may become unable to make decisions about your affairs and your medical treatments. You can have a limited power of attorney assigned to one member of your family to make these decisions while you are incapacitated. The power returns to you when the doctors determine you are able to make your own decisions. Otherwise, someone will have to apply for power of attorney giving them complete power over your affairs and health decisions, and it may not be the person you would have selected. It's good to have this option in place and to discuss your wishes with the person before an emergency occurs.

🔑 Will

This is a very important document every person should have. If you die without a will, the probate judge will disburse your estate. If you are married, you may desire for your spouse to have everything. But in some states, every relative may be entitled to part of your estate where there is no will. Hire a lawyer to properly design a will to your desires. Your estate may change over time so you should be sure to have an updated will included in this package. Providing this information will be very helpful during a stressful time for your family.

PLAN TO PROTECT YOUR FINANCIAL INTEGRITY

🔑 Balance your check book ledger with your bank statement monthly.

Many people get their monthly bank statements and just throw them in the trash or in a file box. If you are guilty of doing this, you are setting yourself up for a financial loss you could have avoided.

One day, I opened up my bank statement and when I saw my bank balance, an alarm went off in my head. I immediately knew something was wrong! I had received a sizeable income tax refund (Note: This was before I made the adjustments to my deductions as I now advise), yet there was little money in my account. My account was short over $3,000! I immediately began to compare my statement with my check ledger and realized the amounts of three checks were grossly different from my ledger. There were three deposits made to my account I had not made. Since this was at a time when the bank would still send me the original checks, I pulled them out of the envelope. Immediately, I could see erasures had been made and the pay to and amounts had been changed. I called the bank and was instructed to immediately come to the main branch in my city. Upon showing the bank representative the checks, they initiated an internal investigation and told me to file a city police report including copies of the checks. Shortly thereafter, they discovered that on three different occasions someone had come to the drive up window of a branch bank in another city and deposited partial checks from an individual made out to me. The checks were made out in different amounts and showed signs of erasures. But in the same transaction, only a small portion of the check was deposited with the balance received as cash. For example, one check was made out for $900 and only $300 was deposited. The bank teller never asked for identification because a deposit was being made and apparently looked at the checks so quickly he or she didn't notice the obvious erasures. The bank representative called me again and told me I had to go to the county and file another police report and bring a copy to the bank because the fraud was committed in another city in the county too. Upon complying with the bank request, the bank corrected my account balance within a few days. I later discovered someone had taken my checks out my mail box and had also done the same thing to someone else. They erased their checks and deposited them in my account and did the same to my checks and deposited them into the other person's account receiving the bulk of the funds as cash. Within weeks, I saw on the news where an arrest was made in another city in another nearby state. The police found boxes of stolen checks.

I was happy the bank had restored my account. However, this incident still cost me as I lost more than a day's wages to comply with the banks requests along with the associated stress. Since this incident, I have seen noticeable changes at all banks on how my transactions are handled. Now, it seems all banks require an ID if you are receiving any funds from an account or inquiring about an account balance even if you have the account number. Make sure you balance your checkbook ledger with your bank statement faithfully every month. I learned another lesson with this incident to protect your financial integrity.

🔑 Don't mail paid bills with checks in them or credit or debit card numbers on the forms from your mailbox.

Your mail box is not safe from thieves! All mail with checks or financial account numbers should be taken to either a locked mail drop box or directly to the Post Office. Checks are not the only thing stolen from the mail. Stolen credit and debit card numbers are possibly a multi-billion dollar business. You must make plans to protect them as well.

🔑 Keep your receipts and balance your monthly credit and debit card statements.

After looking at my monthly credit card statement on another occasion, I realized my credit card had been overdrawn. As I looked at the charges, I saw a charge for over $6,000 that I knew I had not charged. I called the credit card company and found a $6,000 charge was made to a bed and breakfast located in England. The credit card representative told me they would put a fraud alert on the charge and for me not to pay this charge on this month's statement. The representative said they would investigate, and if it was found to be fraud they would remove it from my account within forty-five days. They also mailed and required me to submit a fraud report. Immediately, I looked back at the last three months and found a couple of small charges I did not initiate, and I also reported this to the credit card company and had to file reports on each incident. Note: Like so many others, I had just filed the previous statements in a file box without even looking at them. I later learned these thieves will often make a small charge one month, skip the second month and then wipe you out the third month. They skip the second month to see if you are monitoring your statement. However, some now just max you out immediately.

In addition to filing these reports with the credit card companies, I called the businesses. One of the stores in the United States told me their computer had already detected fraud and was in the process of reversing the charge. It seems the criminal had bought a small amount from them and then when the charges processed they placed an order for a questionable quantity of an item that was very expensive. Thankfully, their computer automatically kicked out the order for a personal review by an associate before actually shipping the items. They had set their computer to do this because fraud was so prevalent and they had lost a lot of money. The other store told me they would review the transaction when they received notification from the credit card company. However, I found fraud charges made outside the United States are not so simple to resolve. Upon speaking with the manager of the bed and breakfast in England about the fraud, he informed me the reservations were made for another month by internet. He also told me he didn't know me and would not consider my request to cancel the reservations even if I sent him evidence that I was who I said I was. I told him if he contacted the police when the person arrived they could investigate and determine that the person was not me. The manager told me that wasn't going to happen. I later learned these criminals will often book reservations like this and never show. They do it for kicks! It doesn't affect them, but you still lose the deposit made to secure the reservations. In this case, it was $6,000. After investigating, the credit card company did determine the charges were fraud and worked it out with the business and then adjusted my account. However, because I was self employed in my business and this card was my business card, I was severely handicapped as I could not use it for more than forty-five days.

While teaching budgeting classes, I have had several testimonies of similar incidents with credit card fraud since this incident happened to me. Another minister in my church as well as my eldest son had similar experiences where charges were made through the internet to companies located in Canada. Credit and debit card fraud is rampant! You must do as follows:

🔑 Protect your account numbers as much as possible.

Use PayPal or similar payment arrangements when possible for internet transactions. If you must use your debit or credit card, make sure the site is well known and protected. Look for complaints on the internet or fraud alerts against the company or website. I can't tell you how many times I've investigated and found problems. Don't commit until you have done your investigation! Don't leave your cards lying around. If a business uses paper transactions that show your account numbers, make sure you get the receipt and duplicates are destroyed once the transaction is completed.

🔑 Keep all your financial information and passwords in a secured place.

Spend the money and purchase a fireproof safe or secure a bank vault to hold all your important documents and passwords. It will be well worth the investment. Let your family know where to find them if there is a need. If it is a bank vault you are using, make sure a family member or trusted friend's name is included on the account with yours in the event of your death or disability that prevents you from accessing the vault.

🗝 Protect your financial information against identity theft.

It is often in the news and perhaps you even know someone who has had their identity stolen. I had a distant family member that said the FBI showed up at his door thinking he was the criminal. He was told a house had been purchased and other accounts had been opened and then monthly payments had not been made by this thief. It is a nightmare to work through this dilemma.

Many companies have rose up, offering identity protection plans for a fee, even the credit bureaus offer plans. But according to all the information I have read on the internet, the reality is even they are limited to what they can do. They monitor your credit reports to see if there is any unusual activity. This is great and works well as long as every creditor, every insurance company, and every apartment complex checks your credit. The fact is all businesses do not contact credit bureaus! Then one day, you are notified you owe debts that never were reported to the credit bureaus. Is this type of protection really worth the cost? Other advisors including me don't think so? Is there a better or cheaper means to give you basically the same protection? Yes, but let me say there are no 100 percent guarantees to protect your credit! The simplest and cheapest way to receive the same protection these companies offer is to simply initiate a security freeze with all the credit bureaus. It is a very simple process you can do in minutes on the internet. Note: Some states do have restrictions, and it is not free in every state to do this. However, the cost is minimal compared to the monthly or annual fees charged by these monitoring companies. If you have been a victim or suspect fraud, you can file fraud protection with the credit bureaus even in states that don't allow freezes.

🔑 **Every adult should initiate a security freeze on their individual credit bureau's file to protect their credit information.**

This means both husband and wife should individually contact the credit bureaus to initiate the freeze on their individual accounts. There are four major credit reporting bureaus: (1) Equifax, (2) TransUnion, (3) Experian, *and (4)* Innovis.[5]

Putting a security freeze on your account only stops new inquiries by businesses you have no association with to check your credit in order to offer you additional credit. Your current associations will still have the right to inquire. When you put this freeze on your account, you will have to plan ahead if you desire to open a new credit account or conduct any business that would involve a credit check. You can temporarily unfreeze and then refreeze your file with the credit bureau. Simply inquire of the business as to which credit bureau they use and then you will need to contact that credit bureau only and file to unfreeze your account. Usually, this must be done three to ten days in advance of the credit report request. Follow the guidelines required by the associated credit bureau to unfreeze and refreeze your account. Note: When you set up to freeze your account online, you will be given a pin number or be asked to give a pin number that will be required for future transactions. Be sure to make paper copies of the information provided along with the pin number and security question and file the information in a fire proof safe or bank vault for future use.

Again, even doing this will not give you a 100 percent guarantee someone will not steal your identity and create credit in your name. It will stop thieves from opening new credit cards or accounts with businesses that inquire with the credit bureaus, but it won't stop it with those that don't inquire. However, along with other prudent actions of protection, this will be good stewardship. You can put a lock on the door, but the thief can still possibly kick the door in or break a window. You can even install a burglar alarm system, but as many have realized, the thief can quickly break in and steal items and be out of the premises prior to the police arriving. Still, this should not stop you from being prudent to protect yourself and your assets within reasonable limits.

Note: Credit freezes will not stop unsolicited credit and insurance offers from businesses inquiring about your credit. These businesses often prescreen your credit score to determine who may be eligible for their products. If you decide you don't want to receive prescreened offers of credit and insurance, you have two choices: you can opt out of receiving them for five years or opt out of receiving them permanently.

To opt out for five years, call toll-free 1-888-5-OPT-OUT (1-888-567-8688) or visit the website [6]The phone number and website are operated by the major consumer reporting companies. To opt out permanently, you may begin the permanent Opt-Out process online. To complete your request, you must return the signed Permanent Opt-Out Election form which will be provided after you initiate your online request.

When you call or visit the website, you'll be asked to provide certain personal information including your home telephone number, name, Social Security number, and date of birth. The information you provide is confidential and will be used only to process your request to opt out.

If you don't have access to the Internet, you may send a written request to permanently opt out to each of the major consumer reporting companies. Make sure your request includes your home telephone number, name, Social Security number, and date of birth.

1. Experian
   Opt Out
   P.O. Box 919
   Allen, TX 75013

2. TransUnion
   Name Removal Option
   P.O. Box 505
   Woodlyn, PA 19094

3. Equifax, Inc.
   Options
   P.O. Box 740123
   Atlanta, GA 30374-0123

4. Innovis Consumer Assistance
   P.O. Box 495
   Pittsburgh, PA 15230-0495

PLAN FOR GIVING

In the beginning, we told you the three biblical purposes for wealth. Those purposes are to help you serve God, to help you meet your needs, and lastly to help you meet the needs of others. We saved the last purpose to end this book!

This third purpose for wealth holds no less importance than using wealth to serve God and to meet our needs. It is God's desire to use you to bless *others*! It is not his desire just for you to bless your family and friends but to also bless the stranger! We see all through Scripture where God instructed his people to take care of the needy and the poor. I personally have found over ninety-three Scriptures dealing with the poor and needy and how

God expects us to respond to them. We can't love God unless we love people! God has given us a plumb line!

> Then shall the King say unto them on his right hand, Come, ye blessed of my Father, inherit the kingdom prepared for you from the foundation of the world For I was an hungred, and ye gave me meat: I was thirsty, and ye gave me drink: I was a stranger, and ye took me in: Naked, and ye clothed me: I was sick, and ye visited me: I was in prison, and ye came unto me. Then shall the righteous answer him, saying, Lord, when saw we thee an hungred, and fed thee? or thirsty, and gave thee drink? When saw we thee a stranger, and took thee in? or naked, and clothed thee? Or when saw we thee sick, or in prison, and came unto thee? And the King shall answer and say unto them, Verily I say unto you, Inasmuch as ye have done it unto one of the least of these my brethren, ye have done it unto me. Then shall he say also unto them on the left hand, Depart from me, ye cursed, into everlasting fire, prepared for the devil and his angels: For I was an hungred, and ye gave me no meat: I was thirsty, and ye gave me no drink: I was a stranger, and ye took me not in: naked, and ye clothed me not: sick, and in prison, and ye visited me not. Then shall they also answer him, saying, Lord, when saw we thee an hungred, or athirst, or a stranger, or naked, or sick, or in prison, and did not minister unto thee? Then shall he answer them, saying, Verily I say unto you, Inasmuch as ye did it not to one of the least of these, ye did it not to me. And these shall go away into everlasting punishment: but the righteous into life eternal.
>
> Matthew 25:34–46 (KJV)

🔑 **When you plan your finances, it must be your goal to fulfill the third priority for wealth in meeting the needs of others.**

In addition, God requires us to give in support of his ministry if we want his blessings. God told his people through the prophet Malachi,

> Will a man rob God? Yet ye have robbed me. But ye say, Wherein have we robbed thee? In tithes and offerings. Ye are cursed with a curse: for ye have robbed me, even this whole nation. Bring ye all the tithes into the storehouse, that there may be meat in mine house, and prove me now herewith, saith the LORD of hosts, if I will not open you the windows of heaven, and pour you out a blessing, that there shall not be room enough to receive it. And I will rebuke the devourer for your sakes, and he shall not destroy the fruits of your ground; neither shall your vine cast her fruit before the time in the field, saith the LORD of hosts. And all nations shall call you blessed: for ye shall be a delightsome land, saith the LORD of hosts.
>
> Malachi 3:8–12 (KJV)

I could spend a whole chapter just expounding on this one passage of Malachi concerning the blessings and curses concerning tithing and giving, but perhaps I will address it in more detail in another book. Let me just say tithing and giving is extremely *important* to God.

Although some believe that tithing was only an Old Testament requirement as part of the Mosaic Law, tithing was set in place long before the Mosaic Law! We see Abraham giving a tithe to Melchizedek in Genesis 14:18 some four hundred years before the Mosaic Law was given. Now where did Abraham learn about tithing? From the Garden of Eden, we see Cain and Able giving and offering to God. Where did they learn this? I believe tithing and giving was passed down from generation to generation prior to Abraham. The Bible does not contain all the history, but it gives us truths so we may understand practices and requirements of God for his people.

I know some believe that tithing was abolished with grace, but we see Jesus declaring:

> Think not that I am come to destroy the law, or the prophets: I am not come to destroy, but to fulfil. For verily I say unto you, Till heaven and earth pass, one jot or one tittle shall in no wise pass from the law, till all be fulfilled.
>
> Matthew 5:17–18 (KJV)

I don't know how it can be any clearer. Jesus himself said he did not destroy the law! What law was he talking about? God's law, the law that includes tithing and giving! The Kings James Bible interprets the Greek word *pleroo* as "fulfil," but it can also be interpreted as satisfy or complete. We know the eighth commandment says, "Thou shalt not kill". But Jesus response was:

> Ye have heard that it was said by them of old time, Thou shalt not kill; and whosoever shall kill shall be in danger of the judgment: But I say unto you, That whosoever is angry with his brother without a cause shall be in danger of the judgment: and whosoever shall say to his brother, Raca, shall be in danger of the council: but whosoever shall say, Thou fool, shall be in danger of hell fire.
>
> Matthew 5:21–22 (KJV)

So what was Jesus doing? He was giving us a deeper spiritual understanding of what God was saying about the commandment not to kill. Thus he was making this commandment complete! He was satisfying God's intent! Do we believe the commandment to kill is dead? Certainly not! Then why do we want to be selective in which commandments to follow? Are all commandments dead? Again, they certainly are *not*!

Likewise, in Matthew 5:17, Jesus was making complete the intent of God's heart. This would explain verse 18 where Jesus says that the law will not pass until all is fulfilled or completed or satisfied. It is like his birth, death, burial, and resurrection were the completion of the atonement process of the Old Testament. Yet, salvation is not really complete until he returns, resurrects the dead in Christ and those alive, and then comes the judgment. Also, Jesus again tells the scribes and Pharisees in:

> Woe unto you, scribes and Pharisees, hypocrites! For ye pay tithe of mint and anise and cummin, and have omitted the weightier matters of the law, judgment, mercy, and faith: these ought ye to have done, and not to leave the other undone.
>
> Matthew 23:23 (KJV)

Notice: He did not tell them to stop tithing. He was giving them a spiritual understanding of God's heart. In addition, Jesus told them what they should have done including the importance of not having left any of these things undone including tithing.

Therefore, with New Testament verification by Jesus and the fact the early church continued the practice of tithing. I can't see anywhere that grace abolished tithing or giving! In fact, we see God blesses when we apply his word of tithing and giving. In the Old Testament, God confirms blessings for tithing and giving. In the New Testament, Jesus says tithing is not abolished, and he confirms blessings with giving.

🔑 You can't out give God!

> Give, and it shall be given unto you; good measure, pressed down, and shaken together, and running over, shall men give into your bosom. For with the same measure that ye mete withal it shall be measured to you again.
>
> Luke 6:38 (KJV)

The New Testament is full of scriptures concerning giving, and we must come to the conclusion that tithing and giving is God's heart and is his intent for the use of wealth. Tithing was God's plan for providing for his ministers, the ministry, and the ministries of the church. This dispensation of God is not complete. We still have ministers, so I don't see where God has released us from providing for them through the tithe.

Now let's address additional giving above the tithe.

🔑 Giving is just as important as tithing to God according to Malachi and Jesus.

I am a strong believer and supporter of giving! However, I may get in trouble with a lot of pastors, but this has been my advice to many couples I have counseled who are in a financial crisis. Pay your tithes, pay your bills, and hold the extra giving until there is extra money beyond your basic needs and current bills. This doesn't give you the liberty to hold onto things you don't need and to continue spending foolishly. You should implement the keys I have given you to quickly get out of debt and then quickly plan to give cheerfully and abundantly.

🔑 God blesses a cheerful giver!

> Every man according as he purposeth in his heart, so let him give; not grudgingly, or of necessity: for God loveth a cheerful giver.
>
> 2 Corithians 9:7 (KJV)

I have counseled people who foolishly gave money in the offering plate or to a TV ministry when they couldn't pay the mortgage or rent or light bill. This violates everything I know about the Scriptures. The only exception is when you know God has spoken to you to give as he did to me in my crisis. Otherwise, get you financial house in order and then develop a plan of giving.

In summary, tithing and giving is one of the greatest methods beyond your personal lifestyle that the individual can use to spread the message of redemption through Jesus Christ. Everyone is not called to be a preacher or a Bible teacher, but everyone can participate in supporting the ministers and the ministry of the Church to fulfill the great commission given by Jesus.

> Go ye therefore, and teach all nations, baptizing them in the name of the Father, and of the Son, and of the Holy Ghost: Teaching them to observe all things whatsoever I have commanded you: and, lo, I am with you always, even unto the end of the world. Amen.
>
> Matthew 28:19–20 (KJV)

In addition, God gives us opportunities to fulfill his commandment to love through the blessings of giving.

IN CONCLUSION

In this book you have received many spiritual and practical keys that God taught Ann and me during our financial crises for getting out of debt and staying out of debt. How we handle finances is a window into our soul. It is a witness as to who is the god of our life. It is extremely important that Christians live within their means. But this book has gone further by sharing spiritual keys that can transform the mind and the spirit to be more like Christ in every aspect of your life. God has called his people to be holy, and we can only be holy because God within us is holy. Everything we think, say, and do declares if God is in us. Do they see God in you? This world is looking for hope. God is the hope for mankind. That hope only comes through the life, shed blood, death, and resurrection of Jesus Christ. If you don't receive anything else out of this book, know that the God of the universe is pursuing you in order to restore a relationship with you. Nothing is by chance; all things are ordained. If you have not received that hope, repent, confess, and commit to give your heart and life to Jesus Christ right now. Ask Jesus to save you! You can experience total freedom, not only from debt but from all bondage. *Get That Monkey off My Back* is a proclamation of spiritual freedom from all bondage. God will do it!

Also, I pray that the God given keys Ann and I shared in this book have been embedded into your mind and spirit, and the Scriptures have cleansed and purified your heart and mind to accept God has a plan for you, and he will give you the wisdom not only to get that debt monkey off your back but to live debt-free! That you might manage his possessions toward his divine will and be an awesome, godly influence on others.

Pray this final prayer,

> Father in heaven, I rejoice in the truth of your word. Your word is a lamp unto my feet and a light unto my path to direct me to become the person to fulfill the purpose for my creation. Keep these truths in my heart, and give me wisdom to implement them according to your divine will. I will bless you and praise you with my mouth and with my daily lifestyle. Use me to bless others! In Jesus's name I pray. Amen!

ADDENDUM

On the following pages are sample forms I use in my counseling classes. You have my permission to use these sample forms for modifying and developing your own spreadsheets.

Explanation of spreadsheets are as follows:

SPENDING WORKSHEET

Most individuals I counsel have no concept of the reality and exactness of their spending. They fill out a life financial plan only later to learn they grossly miscalculated the amounts. Therefore, the first directions I give are to track expenses for the next thirty days on the Spending Worksheet. After thirty days, compare the actual expenses to the initial life financial plan and adjust it accordingly. Often individuals will see areas of spending they can reduce or eliminate simply by looking at the Spending Worksheet. I recommend you keep a note book and envelope in your vehicles to write down expense amounts and to keep receipts. I also recommend keeping a check book register in your vehicles to record any ATM withdrawals and debit card transactions. This will help ensure your amounts are accurate rather than trusting your memory.

INCOME

This sheet will be used to track weekly and monthly income from all sources and provides the useable income for weekly or monthly distribution. Income includes gifts, food stamps, wages, government benefits, etc.

DEBTS

This sheet will provide you one source to refer to in developing your life financial plan and developing a plan to eliminate debt.

Include as much detail as possible when completing the sheet to expedite planning time. Revise this sheet at least quarterly.

ASSETS

This sheet will provide information to determine what assets to liquidate for paying off debts. It also will help determine your net worth. The more detailed information of identified assets, the better judgments you can make. Revise this sheet at least quarterly.

SURVIVAL LIFE FINANCIAL PLAN

Many couples I counsel wait until they are in a desperate financial crisis to seek guidance and counseling. These situations require drastic major financial adjustments. Thus, the first plan we begin using is the survival life financial plan. The survival plan focuses on the basic needs where there are sufficient funds to support the basic needs primarily consisting of food, shelter, medical care, and some form of transportation. The survival plan is just what it implies requiring the elimination of all conveniences and even temporarily some needs as well as finding methods to reduce other expenses. I've counseled individuals who walked to work, church, and shopping because this was the only transportation they could afford. Desperate situations may require temporarily moving in with other family members or down grading to the smallest affordable apartment. When the individual has demonstrated a spirit of humility and has complied with counseling, then it is time first for their blood family and then the church family to assist in the basic needs when family funds are insufficient. To continue counseling, I also require individuals to be faithful in tithing to their local church in order for them to receive God's blessings rather than curses. Additionally, churches assisting a person in financial debt should require the individuals who are able to work to aggressively seek employment and perform volunteer labor for the ministry as directed by the ministers to receive financial assistance from the church. On the survival plan, I do not include church offerings. As previously stated in this book, on the survival plan you can't afford to give an offering and God does not require what you can't give above your tithes. Always the exception to this rule is when you really hear from God and you will know it was God because he will provide the resource to give. Otherwise, during the survival budget only give your tithe.

Often, desperate situations require the husband to secure two jobs, and every able member of the family to secure employment and contribute to the family financial needs.

You will always be in a desperate financial situation until you plan and take action to budget your finances where every expense beyond your basic needs is not a financial crises. Even with survival budgets there should be an effort to begin allocating some available dollars toward the emergency fund. Additionally, assets that the individual can live without should be sold to immediately fund the $1,000 emergency fund account along with finding extra means of producing income. The survival budget should be maintained and gradually adjusted until at least one month of basic living expenses are accumulated in the emergency fund. Only then should you begin to gradually reinstate some of the eliminated items on a life financial plan. Even on the life financial plan, you should continue allocations to the emergency fund account until six months basic livings expenses are accumulated. Then deposit the savings into the general savings and retirement accounts.

The survival life plan and the life financial plan can be weekly or monthly income and expenses. Always use four weeks for determining amounts to enter. If you are paid weekly, I advise using a weekly plan for allocation of income for expenses. Simply divide all monthly bills by four for the weekly plan; divide all quarterly bills by three for the monthly and by twelve for the weekly. Divide all semiannual bills by six for monthly and by twenty-four for weekly plans, divide annual bills by twelve for monthly and by forty-eight for the weekly plan. The extra four weeks will be used to build a surplus in each category or to increase savings. If your weekly income varies, use your previous year tax return and divided the adjusted gross income by twelve to obtain an average monthly income and divide the average monthly income by four for the weekly plan. The goal must be to spend less than you make!

LIFE FINANCIAL PLAN

This form is the next step from the survival plan, except you will use it to expand and address normal family expenses that will occur. Please note all items on the form with * beside them should be added to the amount in the emergency savings until six months' basic living expenses are accumulated and then to the general savings account and transferred to checking only as expenditures are needed. As recommended in the previous chapters, you may have multiple savings accounts for these expenses rather than one general savings account. However, you will plan theses savings using the general savings account. On the sample form the emergency fund account is showing a zero monthly allotment because the six months emergency fund has been met and the savings are now being divided between the general savings and retirement investments accounts. The goal is to plan so spending is less than income so there are sufficient funds for savings and for unallocated funds to be used as God directs you to help others. On this sample form, John and Jane Doe are renting and have planned a fugal lifestyle to see the fulfillment of owning a home come true. Although they owe no money on their car, they continue to make car payments under auto replacement to be able to pay cash for a future replacement vehicle. They opted for a Christian association plan instead of traditional medical insurance. They opted for prepaid minutes on a cell phone over a house phone. They decided to begin investing for retirement now with a small monthly contribution. They also budgeted so there would still be some money unallocated for God to be able to use them to bless others. Note: you will need to budget money for other items such as repairs and replacement of appliances, gifts, vacations, etc. as you pay off your debts as some of these expenses will occur sometime in the future. When filling out your life financial plan after tithes, you must consider basic needs first, savings next and only then you should begin allocating toward non-essential items.

INCOME ALLOCATION

This sheet is used to allocate the weekly or monthly income. You may need to prioritize the categories or even specific items within a category and allocate according to the priority. This is especially true if you are using the survival life financial plan and your average income is less for a week. If your weekly income exceeds the average, first allocate to each category then look to see if a previous category was not funded and then any excess should be allocated to the emergency fund or the general savings.

ACCUMULATIVE EXPENSE

This sheet will be used to track expenses. You will need to fill out a sheet for each category of the Life Financial Plan or if necessary for each expense item under a category. Each week or month you will deposit the budgeted income into the account. Note: Each sheet will be treated like a bank account. Although you will be mindful of your checking and savings accounts, you will operate from the accumulative expense sheets in determining if there are sufficient funds for purchases. Fill out the Budget amount with the appropriate weekly or monthly allocation. Carry balance forward to the next sheet. You can readjust your life financial plan if you find you are being frugal and not spending the allocation amount. These funds can be redirected toward debt or savings or unallocated funds.

CHILD'S INCOME ALLOCATION

It is wise to train a child in the process of budgeting from a young age. Often parents will give their children allowances or allow them to do extra chores for income. The child's income allocation sheet does four things. First, it teaches the child to tithe on income. Second, it teaches the child to save for the future. Third, it teaches the child to give to the needs of others! Fourth, it allows the child to have some immediate spending money to purchase items they desire.

They should also be encouraged to give in the offering plate from their spending money rather than the parent giving them money to put in the plate. The percentages are only suggested amounts. A sheet should be filled out for allocation of income received each week with the child's participation. If the child can write, then let them write in the amounts and count to you the allocation for the savings account. At first, put the savings in a savings bank for the child to see. Once the bank is full or there appears to be a lot of money in the bank, open a bank or credit union savings account in your and the child's name and let them watch the balance grow through bank statements. The above guidelines are for the child's accountability to you and to ensure your wisdom is used to make the right decisions.

YOUNG TEEN INCOME ALLOCATION

This sheet should be used for teens that do tasks for income but have not entered a public job. The percentages are only suggested amounts. This form expands savings to short term items and starts preparing them for saving for future events such as a car, college, home down payment, etc. One sheet should be prepared by the teen for each week's income. Allow the teen to fill in the blanks and go with you to deposit the savings into a bank or credit union account. Keep the sharing money in a bank or jar at home for the young teen to have access to but require them to ask for your permission to distribute or use the money. Let the teen use accumulative expense sheets to allocate short term savings. The above guidelines are for the teen's accountability to you and to ensure your wisdom is used to make the right decisions. At this point in your teens life, you should review your own life financial plan and allow them to see your financial records.

OLDER TEEN INCOME ALLOCATION

This sheet is for the working teen. Again it expands and teaches the teen through home expense sharing to assist parents with household and the teen's expense. If the home expense sharing money is not needed by the parents, it can deposited in a savings account for future life events such as car fund, education, marriage, etc. The percentages are only suggestions. If you have provided transportation to school and work, use the auto section to allow the teen to share in transportation expenses. The teen may not be paying the full amounts, but this will introduce them to real life expenses. If they already have a vehicle that is paid for then divert auto payments to long-term savings. Open a checking account with your and the teen's name and require them to keep the check book register up to date and require them to balance the check book register with the bank statement monthly and review with you. Prior to high school graduation, start working with them in filling out a life financial plan and expense allocation sheets that will go beyond this basic income allocation.

SPENDING WORKSHEET Pg. 1
MONTH: January 2012

DATE	DESCRIPTION	TITHE OFFERING	HOUSING	FOOD	AUTO	INSURANCE	DEBTS	CLOTHING
1/5	Tithe $50, offering $5	$55.00						
1/6	ABC Bank - House Payment		$700.00					
1/8	Zero Mart - groceries			$100.00				
1/9	Grants Clothing - pants/shirt							$42.00
1/10	Tithe $50, offering $5	$55.00						
1/13	Zero Mart - groceries			$100.00				
1/15	City of Hasper - electric bill		$120.00					
1/16	Juno Discount - Bed sheets		$24.00					
1/17	James Hardware - lawn seed		$15.00					
1/18	Sky Insurance - Truck insurance				$467.00			
1/18	Juno - Gas				$65.00			
1/19	Red Charge Card						$55.00	
1/20	Wonder Wild Amuzement Park							$75.00
1/21	Grant Life Company - insurance					$125.00		
	TOTALS	$110.00	$859.00	$200.00	$532.00	$125.00	$55.00	$117.00
			Page Total			$1,998.00		

SPENDING WORKSHEET Pg. 2
MONTH: January 2012

DATE	DESCRIPTION	MEDICAL	MISC:	GIVING	SCHOOL CHILD CARE	SAVINGS	RETIREMENT
1/11	Hair Cut - Wife		$30.00				
1/20	Wonder Wild Amuzement Park		$65.00				
1/21	Dr. James - husband	$65.00					
1/21	K Discount - Medicine husband	$35.00					
1/21	Son's daycare				$125.00		
1/24	Richard Doe			$50.00			
1/25	ABC Bank					$75.00	
1/28	Superior Investments						$100.00
	TOTALS	$100.00	$95.00	$50.00	$125.00	$75.00	$100.00
				Page 2 Total	$545.00		
				Page 1 Total	$1,998.00		
				Grand Total	$2,543.00		

Income

Month: October 2012

DATE	DESCRIPTION	Payroll Gross Pay	Other Income **	Less Payroll Deductions	Net Income	Less Tithe on Gross Income 10%	Useable Income
10/1	Social Security		$600.00		$540.00	$60.00	$480.00
10/1	ABC Cleaning Services	$500.00		$175.00	$325.00	$50.00	$275.00
10/6	Family Assistance		$50.00		$50.00	$5.00	$45.00
10/15	ABC Cleaning Services	$500.00		$175.00	$325.00	$50.00	$275.00
10/20	Family Assistance		$50.00		$50.00	$5.00	$45.00
10/25	Church Assistance		$100.00		$100.00		$100.00
10/26	Salvation Army (Food/Rent)		$50.00		$50.00	$5.00	$50.00
10/27	Gift Card		$25.00		$25.00	$3.00	$22.00
	Totals	$1,000.00	$875.00	$350.00	$1,465.00	$178.00	$1,292.00

**Misc. such as Food Stamps/Family Assistance/Odd Jobs/gift cards

Debts
as of **11/01/09**

TO WHOM OWED	CONTACT NAME PHONE NO.	PAY OFF	PAYMENTS LEFT	MONTHLY PAYMENT	DUE DATE
ABC Bank - house	Ruth Doe -803/366-2012	105000	300	950	1-Nov
Red Credit Card	800/864- 426	2,500	25	100	12-Nov
Blude Credit Card	800/866-4517	5,000	240	100	5-Nov
Sky Furniture - bedroom suite	Joe Doe -803/366-2012	4,000	36	115	20-Nov
Easy Buy Dept. Store - computer	800/646-8374	1,500	12	125	15-Nov
West Credit Union - car	Kay Doe 803/366-4523	8,000	60	375	5-Nov
Mary Doe -Sister		5,000	50	100	5-Nov
Bob Doe - Brother		5,000	50	100	5-Nov
Easy Buy Electronics - TV	800/646-8374	1,200	15	80	20-Nov
Jones Bikes - 4 wheeler	Floyd Doe 803/366-2765	500	5	100	5-Nov
Totals		**137,700.00**		**2,145.00**	

List all debts including family and friends!

Assets

as of 11/01/12

ASSET	CONTACT NAME: PHONE NO.	VALUE	AMOUNT OWED AGAINST
2009 GMC Envoy - West Credit Union	Kay Doe 800/366/5678	12,000	10,000
2001 Ford F250 Truck	Paid for	6,500	0
Misc Furniture	Paid for	1,500	0
House - ABC Bank	Ruth Doe 800/866/6782	125,000	105,000
Wide Screen TV - Easy Buy	Charles Doe 800/487/4260	800	1,200.00
2000 Yamaha 4 wheeler - Jones Bikes	Jones Bikes 800/324-0830	650	500
Washer	Paid for	150	0
Dryer	Paid for	150	0
Dining Room Suite	Paid for	1,000	0
Living Room Suite	Paid for	1,000	0
Mutual Fund - Doe Securities	Ralph Doe 866/324/8765	10,000	0
Savings - West Credit Union	Kay Doe 800/366/5678	2,000	0
Checking - West Credit Union	Kay Doe 800/366/5678	492	0
Cash Surrender Value - Union Life Insurance	Rose Doe 800/444/7829	4,600	0
Bedroom Suite - Sky Furniture	Joe Doe 803/366/2012	4,500	4,000
Computer - Easy Buy	Charles Doe 800/487/4260	1,200	1,500
2010 Buick Car - West Credit Union	Kay Doe 800/366/5678	6,500	8,000
	Totals	178,042	130,200
		Difference	47,842

*List land, buildings, vehicles, savings/checking, retirement accounts, life insurance cash value, stocks, bonds, furniture, vehicles, etc.

Survival Life Financial Plan

NAME: John/Jane Doe   **Date:** 6/30/12

GROSS INCOME		2400.00		**CLOTHING ***		0.00
Salary's	2400					
Interest/Other	0			**MEDICAL**		565.00
				Insurance *	565	
NET INCOME		1968.00		Doctor *	0	
Salary's	1968			Dentist *	0	
Interest/Other	0			Drugs *	0	
				Other Supplies *	0	
LESS Tithe - 10% Gross		240.00				
				MISC.		0.00
NET AVALIABLE INCOME		1728.00		Beauty/Barber	0	
				Laundry/Dry Cleaning	0	
				Subscriptions	0	
EXPENSES				Pocket Money	0	
Housing		650.00		Cell Phones	0	
Mortgage/Rent	500			Internet	0	
Insurance *	0			Vacations/Travel *	0	
Taxes *	0			Movies *	0	
Electricity/Gas	130			Recreation Activities*	0	
Water/Sanitation	20			Other *	0	
Phone	0					
Cable/Satellite	0					
Lawn Care	0			**GIVING**		0.00
Furniture/Appliance*	0			Birthday/Anniversary *	0	
Décor/Equip/Maint. *	0			Family Christmas *	0	
				Others Gifts *	0	
				Church Offerings *	0	
Food		340.00		Other Donations *	0	
Groceries	340					
Dining Out	0			**SCHOOL/CHILD CARE**		0.00
				Tuition *	0	
				Materials *	0	
Automobile		170.00		Transportation *	0	
Payments	0			Day Care	0	
Gas/Oil	125			Misc. *	0	
Insurance	45					
Lic./Taxes *	0			**EMERGENCY FUND ***		3.00
Repairs *	0					
Replacement *	0			**GENERAL SAVINGS ***		0.00
				RETIREMENT INVESTMENTS		0.00
Insurance		0.00				
Life	0			**TOTAL EXPENSES**		1728.00
Special Policies	0					
				INCOME VS. EXPENSES		
				Net Available Income		1728.00
				Less Expenses		1728.00
Debts		0.00				
Credit Cards	0			**UNALLOCATED FUNDS *****		0.00
Loans	0					

* Hold any expense that occurs after 30 days in a savings account until due!

Life Financial Plan

NAME: John/Jane Doe   **Date:** 6/30/12

GROSS INCOME		3760.00		**CLOTHING ***		10.00
Salary's	3750			**MEDICAL**		620.00
Interest/Other	10			Insurance	565	
NET INCOME		3085.00		Doctor *	25	
Salary's	3075			Dentist *	15	
Interest/Other	10			Drugs *	10	
LESS Tithe - 10% Gross		376.00		Other Supplies *	5	
				MISC.		120.00
NET AVALIABLE INCOME		2709.00		Beauty/Barber	20	
				Laundry/Dry Cleaning	0	
EXPENSES				Subscriptions	0	
Housing		795.00		Pocket Money	40	
Mortgage/Rent	560			Cell Phones	35	
Insurance *	20			Internet	0	
Taxes *	0			Vacations/Travel *	25	
Electricity/Gas	130			Movies *	0	
Water/Sanitation	20			Recreation Activities *	0	
Phone	0			Other *	0	
Cable/Satellite	45					
Lawn Care *	0			**GIVING**		60.00
Furniture/Appliance *	10			BirthdayS/Anniversary*	10	
Décor/Equip/Maint. *	10			Family Christmas *	25	
				Others Gifts *	5	
Food		435.00		Church Offerings	20	
Groceries	400			Other Donations *	0	
Dining Out	35					
				SCHOOL/CHILD CARE		0.00
				Tuition *	0	
Automobile		490.00		Materials *	0	
Payments	0			Transportation *	0	
Gas/Oil	150			Day Care	0	
Insurance *	45			Misc. *	0	
Lic./Taxes *	25					
Repairs *	20			**EMERGENCY FUND ***		0.00
Replacement *	250					
				GENERAL SAVINGS *		100.00
				RETIREMENT INVESTMENTS[1]		30.00
Insurance		35.00				
Life	35			**TOTAL EXPENSES**		2695.00
Special Policies	0					
				INCOME VS. EXPENSES		
				Net Available Income		2709.00
Debts		0.00		Less Expenses		2695.00
Credit Cards	0					
Loans	0			**UNALLOCATED FUNDS ***		14.00

* Hold any expense that occurs after 30 days in a savings account until due!

INCOME ALLOCATION
MONTH: AUGUST 2012

Net Monthly Income	3085	Net Weekly Income	771.25	771.25	771.25	771.25	771.25
BUDGET CATEGORY	ALLOCATIONS: MONTHLY	WEEKLY	1ST WEEK	2ND WEEK	3RD WEEK	4TH WEEK	5TH WEEK
1. TITHE	376	94	94	94	94	94	94
2. HOUSING	795	198.75	198.75	198.75	198.75	198.75	198.75
3. FOOD	435	108.75	108.75	108.75	108.75	108.75	108.75
4. AUTO	490	122.5	122.5	122.5	122.5	122.5	122.5
5. INSURANCE	35	8.75	8.75	8.75	8.75	8.75	8.75
6. DEBTS	0	0	0	0	0	0	0
7. CLOTHING	10	2.5	2.5	2.5	2.5	2.5	2.5
8. MEDICAL	620	155	155	155	155	155	155
9. MISC	120	30	30	30	30	30	30
10. GIVING	60	15	15	15	15	15	15
11. SCHOOL/CHILDCARE	0	0	0	0	0	0	0
12. EMERGENCY FUND	0	0	0	0	0	0	0
13. GENERAL SAVINGS	100	25	25	25	25	25	25
14. RETIREMENT	30	7.5	7.5	7.5	7.5	7.5	7.5
15. UNALLOCATED FUNDS	14	3.5	3.5	3.5	3.5	3.5	3.5
TOTALS	2709	771.25	771.25	771.25	771.25	771.25	771.25

Accumulative Expense
Category: **FOOD**
Budget: **$435**

Date	Description	Expense	Deposit	Balance
	Balance Brought Forward:	XXXXXX	XXXXXX	($10)
2-Jul	Weekly Deposit		$108.75	$98.75
6-Jul	ABC groceries	$85.00		$13.75
6-Jul	Franks groceries	$12.00		$1.75
9-Jul	Weekly Deposit		$108.75	$110.50
13-Jul	ABC groceries	$95.00		$15.50
13-Jul	Franks groceries	$15.00		$0.50
16-Jul	Weekly Deposit		$108.75	$109.25
20-Jul	ABC groceries	$75.00		$34.25
20-Jul	Franks groceries	$10.00		$24.25
23-Jul	Weekly Deposit		$108.75	$133.00
27-Jul	ABC groceries	$65.00		$68.00
27-Jul	Great Food Restaurant	$35.00		$33.00
30-Jul	Weekly Deposit		$108.75	$141.75
	Totals	$392.00	$543.75	$141.75

CHILD'S INCOME ALLOCATION

GROSS INCOME	**$25.00**
LESS 10% TITHE	**$2.50**
NET SPENDABLE INCOME	**$22.50**
SAVINGS (50%)	**$11.25**
SPENDING MONEY (40%) (special wants, church offerings)	**$9.00**
SHARING MONEY (10%) (Giving to needs of others)	**$2.25**

Young Teen Income Allocation

GROSS INCOME $25.00

LESS TITHE $2.50

NET SPENDABLE INCOME $22.50

SHORT TERM SAVINGS (25%) $5.63
  (Events that will happen within the next 12 months like vacations, special wants, clothing,)

LONG TERM SAVINGS (40%) $9.00
  (Events that will happen over a longer period of time like Car, land/home, college, etc.)

POCKET MONEY (30%) $6.75
  (Events that will happen within next 30 days like small items, refreshments, church offerings, etc.)

SHARING MONEY (5%) $1.12
  (Giving to needs of others)

OLDER TEEN INCOME ALLOCATION

GROSS INCOME		**$200.00**
LESS TITHE	**$20.00**	
LESS PAYROLL DEDUCTIONS	**$30.00**	
NET SPENDABLE INCOME		**$150.00**
HOME EXPENSE SHARING (15%)		**$22.50**

(Optional: to be used to help with household expense or can put into a educational fund, marriage, or car fund)

SHORT TERM SAVINGS (5%) — **$7.50**
(Events that will happen within the next 12 months like vacations, special wants, clothing)

LONG TERM SAVINGS (7%) — **$10.50**
(Events that will happen over a longer period of time like Car, land/home, college, etc.)

POCKET MONEY (10%) — **$15.00**
(Events that will happen within next 30 days like dates, small items, refreshments, eating out, church offerings, beauty, barber, laundry)

AUTOMOBILE (60%) — **$90.00**

Payments	$40.00
Gas & Oil	$25.00
Insurance	$10.00
License/Taxes	$2.00
Maint./Repair/Replace	$13.00

SHARING MONEY (3%) — **$4.50**
(To be used as given inspiration by God)

ENDNOTES

1. Life Ministries of Rock Hill: LifeMinistries.ministries@gmail.com or gwpike@comporium.net.

2. Christian Care Medi-Share: www.medi-share.org.

3. Partnership for Prescription Assistance: www.pparx.org/en/prescription_assistance_programs

4. RX Outreach: www.rxoutreach.org

5. Equifax: www.equifax.com; TransUnion: www.transunion.com; Experian: www.experian.com; Innovis: www.innovis.com.

6. www.optoutprescreen.com.